D0890135

That All Shall Be Saved

That All Shall Be Saved

Heaven, Hell, and Universal Salvation

DAVID BENTLEY HART

Yale UNIVERSITY PRESS

New Haven and London

Published with assistance from the Louis Stern Memorial Fund.

Yale University Press books may be purchased in quantity for educational, business, or promotional use. For information, please e-mail sales.press@yale.edu (U.S. office) or sales@yaleup.co.uk (U.K. office).

Set in Minion type by Tseng Information Systems, Inc., Durham, North Carolina.
Printed in the United States of America.

Library of Congress Control Number: 2019933695
ISBN 978-0-300-24622-3 (hardcover : alk. paper)

A catalogue record for this book is available from the British Library.

This paper meets the requirements of ANSI/NISO Z39.48-1992 (Permanence of Paper).

10 9 8 7 6 5 4 3 2 1

For Narcis Tasca,
who reminded me of something that I was
in imminent danger of forgetting,
though it was something of the utmost importance

"Our savior God . . . intends that all human beings shall be saved and come to a full knowledge of the truth."

—1 TIMOTHY 2:3–4

Contents

Introduction

There have been Christian "universalists"—Christians, that is, who believe that in the end all persons will be saved and joined to God in Christ—since the earliest centuries of the faith. In fact, all the historical evidence suggests that the universalist faction was at its most numerous, at least as a relative ratio of believers, in the church's first half millennium. Augustine of Hippo (354–430) referred to such persons as *misericordes*, "the merciful-hearted," an epithet that for him apparently had something of a censorious ring to it (one, I confess, that is quite inaudible to me). In the early centuries they were not, for the most part, an especially eccentric company. They cherished the same scriptures as other Christians, worshipped in the same basilicas, lived the same sacramental lives. They even believed in hell, though not in its eternity; to them, hell was the fire of purification described by the Apostle Paul in the third chapter of 1 Corinthians, the healing assault of unyielding divine love upon obdurate souls, one that will save even those who in this life prove unworthy of heaven by burning away every last vestige of their wicked deeds. The universalists were not even necessarily at first a minority among the faithful, at least not everywhere. The great fourth-century church father Basil of Caesarea (c. 329–379) once observed that, in his time, a large majority of his fellow Christians (at least, in the Greek-speaking Eastern Christian world that he knew) believed that hell was not everlasting, and that all in the end would attain salvation. This may have been hyperbole on his part, but then again it may very well not have been; and, even if he was exaggerating, he could not have been exaggerating very much, as otherwise the remark would have sounded silly to his contemporaries, whereas he stated the matter as something almost banal in its obviousness. Over time, of course, in large part as a result of certain obvious institutional imperatives, the voices of the universalists would dwindle away to little more than a secretive whisper at the margins of the faith, except in a few of the sunnier quarters of Christendom (such as the East Syrian church). And it was not, perhaps, until the nineteenth century that the tide of opinion on this matter began, if only ever so slightly, to turn back again.

Much of what I shall argue in this book, consequently, is likely to seem rather exotic to many readers, and perhaps even a little perverse. But this would not have been the case in, say, the first four centuries of the church, especially not in the eastern half of the Roman imperial world and its neighboring territories, precisely because the believers of those times and places were closer to the culture, language, cosmology, and religious expectations of the apostolic age; as yet, their imaginations had not been corrupted by centuries of theology written in entirely different spiritual and intellectual environments, and in alien tongues. My chief ambition in what follows, therefore, is to try to think through certain questions about "the last things" in a way that might naturally bring me nearer to the obscure origins of the Christian conception of reality, when the earliest texts of Christian scripture were still being written, edited, sorted through, and designated as either canonical or spurious. My hope is that I can assume a vantage somehow "innocent" of any number of presuppositions belonging to the inheritance of later developments in Christian culture. In a sense, in fact, I regard this book as a companion to, or additional piece in the critical apparatus of, my recent *The New Testament: A Translation* (Yale University Press, 2017). If possible (and I say this not *simply* in the hope of further increasing my sales), I hope the reader of this book can consult also the introduction and postscript of that volume, and perhaps the footnotes it provides for some of the verses cited here. Perhaps he or she might even read the translation in its entirety (I can vouch, if nothing else, for the good faith of the translator). I am firmly convinced that two millennia of dogmatic tradition have created in the minds of most of us a fundamentally misleading picture of a great many of the claims made in Christian scripture. And I hope that my translation— simply by restoring certain ambiguities I believe to be present in the original texts—might help modern readers understand how it is that a considerable number of educated late antique Eastern Christians, all of whom were familiar with the New Testament in the original Greek, felt entirely comfortable with a universalist construal of its language. It is my conviction, you see, that the *misericordes* have always been the ones who got the story right, to the degree that it is true at all. That is not to say that they were all in perfect agreement with one another, or that I am in perfect agreement with all of them regarding every aspect of that story. I mean only that, if Christianity taken as a whole is indeed an entirely coherent and credible system of belief, then the universalist understanding of its message is the only one possible. And, quite imprudently, I say that without the least hesitation or qualification.

I find it a very curious feeling, I admit, to write a book
that is at odds with a body of received opinion so invincibly
well-established that I know I cannot reasonably expect to per-
suade anyone of anything, except perhaps of my sincerity. The
whole endeavor may very well turn out to be pointless in the
end. I suspect that those who are already sympathetic to my
position will approve of my argument to the extent that they
think it successfully expresses their own views, or something
proximate to them, while those who disagree (by far the larger
party) will either dismiss it or (if they are very boring indeed)
try to refute it by reasserting the traditional majority position
in any number of very predictable, very shopworn manners.
Some, for instance, will claim that universalism clearly contradicts the explicit language of scripture (it does not). Others will
argue that universalism was decisively condemned as hereti-
cal by the fifth Ecumenical Council (it was not). The more ad-
venturous will attempt what they take to be stronger versions
of those same philosophical defenses of the idea of an eternal
hell that I describe and reject in these pages. The most adven-
turous of all might attempt to come up with new arguments
of their own (which is not advisable). There is no obvious way
of winning at this game, or even of significantly altering the
odds. Even so, I intend to play it to the end. And perhaps I
can derive a certain comfort from my situation. There is, at
the very least, something liberating about knowing that I have
probably lost the rhetorical contest before it has even begun.
It spares me the effort of feigning tentativeness or moderation
or judicious doubt, in the daintily and soberly ceremonious
way one is generally expected to do, and allows me instead to
advance my claims in as unconstrained a manner as possible,
and to see how far the line of reasoning they embody can be
pursued. For all I know, this in itself might make some kind of

worthwhile contribution to the larger conversation, even if in the end it should prove to be a suasive failure; if nothing else, this book may provide champions of the dominant view an occasion for honest reflection and scrupulous cerebration and serious analysis (and a whole host of other bracing intellectual virtues of that sort). Even if it should serve merely as a kind of negative probation of the tradition—the plaintiff's brief dutifully submitted by an *advocatus diaboli,* on behalf of an eccentric minority position, in full anticipation that the final verdict will go the other way—it may at least help the majority to clarify their convictions. So, I offer all that follows as a logical and rhetorical experiment, and ask chiefly for the reader's indulgence as I proceed as far along the path of my reasoning as I find it possible to go. My expectations regarding its effect are very limited. Even so, if by chance the reader should happen to find any of my arguments convincing after all, I ask also that he or she consider whether that might be the result of some intrinsic merit in them.

I should note that this is not the first public exposition of my views, but I intend it to be more or less the last. In my experience, this particular issue is especially fertile in generating circular debates, and in inviting the most repetitious sorts of argument. But I feel I have to give a complete account of my views on the matter simply as a courtesy to those who have taken the time to respond to my earlier statements, but without the benefit of knowing the entire shape of my thinking. Back in July 2015, at the University of Notre Dame, I delivered a lecture, most of whose argument is reprised below in my First Meditation. At the time, it received considerable attention, and it continues to provoke discussion and commentary in various venues. Many readers have followed its argument without difficulty, usually with approbation, probably on account of a prior disposition on their parts to agree with something like my general approach to these matters. There were other, less enthusiastic reactions as well, however. Regarding these, though, I can honestly say that, to this point, all have been based on misunderstandings — sometimes extravagant — of my lecture's central contentions. This is not, I think, because what I said that day was particularly difficult to follow, but rather because I did not advance the conventional argument that many critics quite reasonably expected me to make, and so they reflexively read into my words the one they were already prepared to reject. As a consequence, I have been asked repeatedly in the past few years to answer objections to positions I have never taken. The only good thing I can report about this is that I seem to have nearly perfected a tone of voice that veils vexation behind lustrous clouds of disingenuous patience; and the acquisition of a new social skill is always a blessing. But otherwise, to tell the truth, this is just the sort of conversation that makes the pleasure of even the most charming soiree begin to pall; I mean, really, how many times can one say, "I'm sorry, you've mistaken me for someone else" before the siren song of the cocktail-shaker across the room becomes irresistible, or before one suddenly remembers that one is extremely late for a pressing appointment one has made with the large topiary duck in the garden? So it is my hope that here, in company with the rest of my argument, the questions I raised and points I made in that earlier, more fragmentary presentation will be so clear as to require no further elaboration. Then the argument as a whole may instead, I hope, simply be accepted or rejected or ignored, as the reader pleases. But, for me at least, debate is otiose. For better or worse, my reasoning convinces me entirely, and that — sadly or happily — will certainly never change.

I

The Question of an Eternal Hell

Alice laughed. "There's no use trying," she said: "one *can't* believe impossible things."

"I daresay you haven't had much practice," said the Queen. "When I was your age, I always did it for half-an-hour a day. Why, sometimes I've believed as many as six impossible things before breakfast."

—LEWIS CARROLL, *THROUGH THE LOOKING-GLASS*

Framing the Question

According to a legend recounted in the *Apophthegmata Patrum,* or *Sayings of the Fathers*—a name shared in common by various ancient Christian collations of anecdotes about the Egyptian "desert fathers" of the fourth century—the holy man Abba Macarius (c. 300–391) was walking alone in the wilderness one day when he came upon a human skull lying beside the path and, as he casually moved it aside with his staff, it all at once began to utter words. Astonished, Macarius asked it to identify itself, and it obliged. It told him that in life it had been a pagan high priest who had tended the idols and performed the rites of the people that had once dwelled in those climes. It said also that it recognized Macarius, and knew him to be a bearer of the Spirit, one whose prayers actually had the power temporarily to ease the sufferings of the damned. Hearing this, Macarius asked the skull to describe those sufferings. It replied that he and his fellow pagans were forced to stand crowded together, day and night, wrapped from head to foot in flames, suspended above an abyss of fire stretching as far below their feet as the sky had stretched above their heads when they had lived upon the earth. Moreover, it added, they were prevented even from looking one another in the face; their eyes had been eternally fixed each upon his neighbor's back. And yet, added the skull, whenever Macarius prayed for those poor lost souls, they found themselves momentarily able to glimpse the faces of their fellows after all, for which they were profoundly grateful; for this was the only respite they could ever hope to enjoy amid their unrelenting torments. On hearing these things, Macarius began to weep, and declared that it would have been better had the unfortunate priest never been born at all. He then asked whether there were others in hell enduring even greater tortures than these, and the skull told him that indeed there were. In fact, it said, the suffering visited on him and his fellow pagans was comparatively mild, since they had never known the true God and so had never really had the choice of serving him; immeasurably more terrible were the penalties endured by those plunged deep down in the abyss of fire below, it said, for they *had* known God and had rejected him nevertheless. In dread, Macarius buried the skull and hastened on his way.

I was, I think, fourteen when I first read that story, in a volume of writings from the early church belonging to my eldest brother. I was not a particularly pious youth, but I liked old legends. And then, a week or so later, quite by coincidence, I heard the same story recited in a sermon by an Episcopal priest (exceedingly high church), who seemed to fall into something like a mystic transport as he rhapsodized upon the tale's rare beauty: the deftly minimalist skill with which it painted its portrait of the merciful soul of Abba Macarius, the ravishingly lovely conceit that even the pains of hell may be alleviated by the sight of another human face, the piercing reminder that our pity must admit no boundaries (and other things along those lines). For the life of me, I had no idea what he was talking about. My reactions to the story had been entirely different, on both occasions. To me, it had been no more than a conventional ghost story, one whose atmosphere of the fantastically dismal was all that accounted for whatever small, ghastly charm it possessed. And I had certainly read enough folklore, from many lands and many religions, to think I could recognize the type of narrative it was (though at the time the exact description would probably have eluded me): a rustic fable, meant to terrify refractory children and credulous peasants, and marked by that casual callousness that is so frequent a concomitant of deep piety. Not for a moment, as far as I can recall, had it occurred to me to take the story seriously, or to think that it had anything to tell me either about God or about the life to come. True, I had approved of the tears that Abba Macarius had shed for the damned, and of his compassionate, albeit fruitless, gesture of according the skull a decent interment. But that was the extent of the tale's human appeal for me. Even before that Episcopal priest had reached the end of his sermon, I realized that, if he really wanted me to treat the story as a serious parable of the faith, the result was not going to be the one he intended. My principal reaction to it in those terms would have been perplexity at a fable that seemed to say—and with so little evasion—that Abba Macarius was not only extraordinarily merciful, but in fact immeasurably more merciful than the God he worshipped. It would also have been exceedingly hard for me not to notice how viciously vindictive the creator of such a hell would have had to be to have devised so exquisitely malicious a form of torture and then to have made it eternal, and how unjust in condemning men and women to unending torment for the "sin" of not knowing him even though he had never revealed himself to them, or for some formally imputed guilt supposedly attaching to them on account of some distant ancestor's transgression. For me, the tale's ultimate lesson would have had to be the one that Macarius himself had uttered: "Alas that such a man was ever born!" After all, I concluded in my juvenile way, if God knows all things, and so knew from everlasting that the final fate of the high priest would be to suffer everlasting torment, then the very choice to create him had been an act of limitless cruelty.

I ignored the sermon in any event, as I tended to do with most sermons in those days (and still tend to do today, to be honest). As I say, I was not particularly devout. But, while the story itself failed to leave a very deep impression on my thinking, the conclusion I had reached as a result of the sermon that day remained with me, and I have never really wavered from it since then. I still find myself unable to repudiate my initial, callow response: a slight shiver of distaste at the naïve religious mind at its most morally obtuse, and then boredom at what I took to be an inept attempt to scare me. I had seen a few badly made horror films on television, after all. Since then, admittedly, I have encountered far subtler pictures of perdition and, at tedious length, have mastered all of the more common arguments for the moral intelligibility of the idea of a hell of eternal torment, not to mention a good number of the uncommon ones. None of these, however, has ever persuaded me of anything, except perhaps the lengths of specious reasoning to which even very intelligent persons can go when they feel bound by faith to believe something inherently incredible. And, to be honest, even if any versions of those arguments did seem plausible to me, they would still fail to move me, since no versions deal adequately with the actual question that to me seems the most obvious and most crucial—at least, if one truly believes that Christianity offers any kind of cogent picture of reality. The great majority of defenders of the idea of a real hell of eternal torment (for brevity's sake, we can call them "infernalists" hereafter) never really get around to addressing properly the question of whether we can make moral sense of God's acts in the great cosmic drama of creation, redemption, and damnation. They invariably imagine they have done so, but only because they have not sufficiently distinguished that question from whichever one it is that genuinely preoccupies them—which these days tends to be the question of whether a free, rational agent, in order to be *truly* free, or *truly* capable of a relation of love with God, must have the power justly to condemn himself or herself to everlasting dereliction, and whether then God will allow him or her to do so out of regard for the high dignity of this absolutely indispensable autonomy. That is a perfectly interesting line of inquiry in its own right, I suppose, or appears to be on its surface so long as one accepts its premises, and it is in fact one that I discuss at some length in the meditations that compose the greater part of this book; but it remains, to my mind, a subordinate issue. No matter how one answers that particular question, the always more significant question must be whether—even if it should turn out that a rational soul really can in some abstract sense freely and justly condemn itself to everlasting torture—this fact would truly permit us to love an omnipotent and omniscient God who has elected to create a reality in which everlasting torture is a possible final destiny for any of his creatures. (Do not respond yet, incidentally, especially not if you want to say yes; anyone who assumes that the correct answer is easy or obvious has not, in all likelihood, quite grasped the full logical depths of the problem.)

I should probably note that I may have been predisposed to react to the tale of Macarius and the skull as I did by early exposure to influences from entirely outside Christian tradi-

tion (which, no doubt, some would regard as unhealthy). Even
at that tender age, I had already been fascinated with Asian lit-
eratures, cultures, and religions for years, and knew that this
would constitute some significant portion of my future scholarly and literary interests. I suspect it all started very early in
childhood, with a large anthology of classical Indian and Chinese texts edited by Lin Yutang that was one of my especially
prized books as a boy, as well as several volumes of Lafcadio
Hearn (the ghost stories in particular), various collections of
Asian myths and legends and poems, and such condensed versions of the great Indian epics as were available at the time
(and, I have to admit, the television program *Kung Fu* had
something of a powerful influence over me at an impression-
able age). I had even come by then to know quite a lot about
the Mahayana Buddhist understanding of bodhisattvas: those
fully enlightened saviors who could, if they chose, enter finally
into the unconditioned bliss of Nirvana, but who have instead
vowed not to do so until all other beings have been gathered
in before them, and who therefore, solely out of their super-
abounding compassion, strive age upon age for the liberation
of all from Samsara, the great sea of suffering and ignorance.
They even vow to pass through and, if need be, endure the
pains of all the many *narakas,* those horridly numerous and
ingeniously terrifying Buddhist hells, in pursuit of the lost. But
then, in fact, in a marvelous and radiant inversion of all expectations, it turns out that such compassion is itself already the
highest liberation and beatitude, and that, seen in its light, the
difference between Samsara and Nirvana simply vanishes. Of
course, I was too young as yet to have understood the more re-
condite details of the various schools of Buddhist thought, and
certainly had not yet read any of the more difficult texts on the
figure of the bodhisattva, such as Śantideva's glorious *Bodhi-*

caryavatara; but it did not take any great academic sophistica-
tion on my part to be able to see the vast moral beauty in the
very idea of such a figure. And yet I knew I was not a Buddhist,
and had no imminent anticipation of becoming one; and so,
being naturally competitive, I also found the idea slightly troubling. It made me anxious that Christians were in danger of
being outdone in the "love and mercy" department by other
creeds. Hence, as I say, I was perhaps already prepared to see
the Macarius legend in a somewhat off-kilter manner. It would
have been very hard for me to accept the thought that the "infinite love" and "omnipotent benevolence" of the Christian
God would ultimately prove immeasurably less generous or
effectual than the "great compassion" and "expedient means"
of the numberless, indefatigably merciful bodhisattvas popu-
lating the Mahayana religious imagination. And it would have
been positively chilling to me to think that Christ's harrowing
of hades was, by comparison to the unremitting campaign of
universal rescue conducted by the saviors of Buddhism, little
more than a limited reconnaissance and relief mission.

I may, in retrospect, have been at that period very near
to concluding that Christianity was too morally confused and
distasteful a religion to be accorded any real credence. It was
perhaps solely out of my loyalty to my father's very deep faith
that I did not abandon the whole enterprise some time in my
late teens. And then, over the next few years, especially as I
pursued my undergraduate studies in world religions, things
became a bit easier; and much of my anxiety was alleviated as I
came better to know the larger and more diverse Christian tradition of reflection on the destiny of souls. At least, it became
possible for me to believe that there were streams within the
tradition that seemed to make real moral sense of the notion of
hell. From an early age (I cannot quite recall which), I had been

drawn to Eastern Christianity much more powerfully than to its Western counterparts. One of the advantages of growing up high Anglican is that one is often exposed to the Eastern church fathers even in childhood, and for some reason I came very early to feel, fairly or not, that Christianity not only had arisen in Hellenistic and Semitic lands, but also had in all likelihood never entirely succeeded in spreading beyond them in a pure form (at least, in a westward direction). And, as I continued to explore the Eastern communions as an undergraduate, I learned at some point to take comfort from an idea that one finds liberally scattered throughout Eastern Christian contemplative tradition, from late antiquity to the present, and expressed with particular force by such saints of the East as Isaac of Nineveh (c. 613–c. 700) and Silouan of Athos (1866–1938): that the fires of hell are nothing but the glory of God, which must at the last, when God brings about the final restoration of all things, pervade the whole of creation; for, although that glory will transfigure the whole cosmos, it will inevitably be experienced as torment by any soul that willfully seals itself against love of God and neighbor; to such a perverse and obstinate nature, the divine light that should enter the soul and transform it from within must seem instead like the flames of an exterior chastisement.

This I found not only comforting, but also extremely plausible at an emotional level. It is easy to believe in that version of hell, after all, if one considers it deeply enough, for the very simple reason that we all already know it to be real in this life, and dwell a good portion of our days confined within its walls. A hardened heart is already its own punishment; the refusal to love or be loved makes the love of others—or even just their presence—a source of suffering and a goad to wrath. At the very least, this is a psychological fact that just about any of us can confirm from experience. And, surely, if the soul does live on past the grave, as faith claims it does, it must carry the hell that it has nurtured within itself into the next world. And so, perhaps, it makes perfect sense to imagine that a will sufficiently intransigent in its selfishness and resentment and violence might be so damaged that, even when fully exposed to the divine glory for which all things were made, it will absolutely hate the invasion of that transfiguring love, and will be able to discover nothing in it but terror and pain. It is the soul, then, and not God, that lights hell's fires, by interpreting the advent of divine love as a violent assault upon the jealous privacy of the self. I was briefly content with this way of seeing things. It seemed to explain the matter quite tidily, without question. But, in the end, I concluded that even this account of the matter was plausible only up to a point. And, to tell the truth, that point is not one that is hard to reach. Once one has had time to think about it for a little while, one should notice that, when all is said and done, this very rational and psychologically plausible understanding of hell still in no significant way improves the larger picture of God as creator and redeemer—at least, not if one insists upon adding the qualification "eternal" or "final" to the condition of self-imposed misery that it describes. At that point, we find that our two questions remain as gallingly unaddressed as ever: the secondary question of whether this defiant rejection of God for all of eternity is really logically possible for any rational being; and the primary question of whether the God who creates a reality in which the eternal suffering of any being is possible—even if it should be a self-induced suffering—can in fact be the infinitely good God of love that Christianity says he is. (Again, do not try to answer yet.)

II

One argument that I shall make in this book is that the very notion that a rational agent in full possession of his or her faculties could, in any meaningful sense, freely reject God absolutely and forever is a logically incoherent one. Another is that, for this and other reasons, a final state of eternal torment could be neither a just sentence pronounced upon nor a just fate suffered by a finite being, no matter how depraved that being might have become. Still another is that, even if that fate were in some purely abstract sense "just," the God who would permit it to become anyone's *actual* fate could never be perfectly good—or, rather, as Christian metaphysical tradition obliges us to phrase it, could never be absolute Goodness as such—but could be at most only a relative calculable good in relation to other relative calculable goods. And yet another is that the traditional doctrine of hell's perpetuity renders other aspects of the tradition, such as orthodox Christology or the eschatological claims of the Apostle Paul, ultimately meaningless. If all of this seems obscure, which at this point it should, I hope it will have become clear by the end of the book. I cannot be certain that it will have done so, however, because Christians have been trained at a very deep level of their thinking to believe that the idea of an eternal hell is a clear and unambiguous element of their faith, and that therefore the idea *must* make perfect moral sense. They are in error on both counts, as it happens, but a sufficiently thorough conditioning can make an otherwise sound mind perceive even the most ostentatiously absurd proposition to be the very epitome of rational good sense. In fact, where the absurdity proves only slight, the mind that has been trained most thoroughly will, as often as not, fabricate further and more extravagant absurdities, in order to secure the initial offense against reason within a more encompassing and intoxicating atmosphere of corroborating nonsense. Sooner or later, it will all seem to make sense, simply through ceaseless repetition and restatement and rhetorical reinforcement. The most effective technique for subduing the moral imagination is to teach it to mistake the contradictory for the paradoxical, and thereby to accept incoherence as profundity, or moral idiocy as spiritual subtlety. If this can be accomplished with sufficient nuance and delicacy, it can sustain even a very powerful intellect for an entire lifetime. In the end, with sufficient practice, one really can, like the White Queen, learn to believe as many as six impossible things before breakfast.

Not that I am accusing anyone of consciously or cynically seeking to manipulate the minds of faithful Christians. The conspiracy, so to speak, is an entirely open one, an unpremeditated corporate labor of communal self-deception, requiring us all to do our parts to sustain one another in our collective derangement. I regard the entire process as the unintentional effect of a long tradition of error, one in which a series of bad interpretations of scripture produced various corruptions of theological reasoning, which were themselves then preserved as immemorial revealed truths and, at the last, rendered impregnable to all critique by the indurated mental habits of generations—all despite the logical and conceptual incongruities that this required believers to ignore within their beliefs. So I really do take all parties at their words. For instance, I think that traditional Thomists are entirely sincere when they argue that God could not have forborne to create souls he had predestined to eternal torment, and certainly could never now allow them peacefully to lapse again into nonexistence, on the

grounds that it would constitute a kind of parsimony or jeal-
ousy on his part to withhold the gift of being—a gift he possesses in infinite plenitude—from anyone. For the Thomist,
being is the first good, higher than any other, inasmuch as
God himself is subsistent Being, and so, even for a soul in hell,
nonexistence would be a greater evil than perpetual agony. Of
course, this is ridiculous; but it helps fill in one of the gaps in
the tale. A gift that is at once wholly irresistible and a source of
unrelieved suffering on the part of its recipient is not a gift at
all, even in the most tenuously analogous sense; and, speaking
for myself, I cannot see how existence as such is truly a divine
gift if it has been entirely severed from free and rational participation in the goodness of things. Being itself is the Good
itself, no doubt. But, for creatures who exist only by finite participation in the gift of existence, only well-being is being-
as-gift in a true and meaningful sense; mere bare existence is
nothing but a brute fact, and often a rather squalid one at that,
and to mistake it for an ultimate value is to venerate an idol
(call it the sin of "hyparxeolatry," the worship of subsistence
in and of itself, of the sort that misers and thieves and those
who would never give their lives for others commit every day).

That, admittedly, is open to debate. But, then again,
there precisely lurks the problem: The entire matter is debatable through and through. What I find fascinating about the
Thomist position here is not that it is "wrong"—it does not
rise to the level of the correct or incorrect—but that it is utterly
devoid of so much as a trace of compelling logical content. It
poses its own premises not as logically established or analytic
truths, but simply as necessary correlates of its own foregone
conclusions. The argument is nothing but a naked assertion,
one that can recommend itself favorably only to a mind that
has already been indoctrinated in obedience to a much larger

and more pernicious set of assumptions, and that has been prepared by a long psychological and dogmatic formation to accept ludicrous propositions without complaint if it must, as it gropes about for justifications for a much more ludicrous system of belief it feels it cannot reject. And what could be more absurd than the claim that God's ways so exceed comprehension that we dare not presume even to distinguish benevolence from malevolence in the divine, inasmuch as either can result in the same endless excruciating despair? Here the docile believer is simply commanded to nod in acquiescence, quietly and submissively, to feel moved at a strange and stirring obscurity, and to accept that, if only he or she could sound the depths of this mystery, its essence would somehow be revealed as infinite beauty and love. A rational person capable of that assent, however—of believing all of this to be a paradox concealing a deeper, wholly coherent truth, rather than a gross contradiction—has probably suffered such chronic intellectual and moral malformation that he or she is no longer able to recognize certain very plain truths: such as the truth that he or she has been taught to approve of divine deeds that, were they reduced to a human scale of action, would immediately be recognizable as expressions of unalloyed spite.

Then again, I suppose that we are all susceptible to rhetorical sorceries of this kind, at one time or another. I, for example, have found myself genuinely fascinated and moved on various occasions by the words that Dante—at least, the Dante who is the protagonist of the *Commedia*—saw inscribed in dark letters above the gates of hell:

> Per me si va ne la città dolente,
>   per me si va ne l'etterno dolore,
>   per me si va tra la perduta gente.

Giustizia mosse il mio alto fattore;
    fecemi la divina podestate,
    la somma sapïenza e 'l primo amore.
Dinanzi a me non fuor cose create
    se non etterne, e io etterno duro.
    Lasciate ogne speranza, voi ch'intrate.

                                   (*Inferno* III.1–9)

(Through me lies the way into the sorrowful city, /
through me lies the way to eternal misery, / through
me lies the way that passes through the lost people. /
Justice moved my Father on high; / I was fashioned
by divine power, / highest wisdom, and primal
love. / There were no things created before me, /
Save those that are eternal, and I eternally endure: /
Abandon every hope, you who enter in.)

Fashioned by primal love. I cannot even guess how often I have
heard those words repeated as an example of some wonder-
ful or terrible paradox of the faith, one that tells us something
astonishingly and miraculously true and profound about the
high, vertiginous dignity of being created in the divine image,
and thus of being granted the power to choose "this very day"
between good and evil, life and death. We see this mystery
played out, supposedly, in the way that each of the punishments Dante observes being inflicted upon the damned is not
only a fitting recompense for that particular sinner's special
transgressions, but fitting precisely because it is clearly in some
sense a self-imposed penalty; each chastisement is an inverted
expression of the violence that the sinner worked upon the
world during his or her life, and thereby worked upon himself
or herself in eternity. Divine mercy, you see, has provided an

arena of moral freedom, so the story goes, one in which every fallen soul can become fully what it has chosen to be. And so there really is a logic of love at work here, a kind of divine magnanimity. The soul that prefers having hell to surrendering to God's love receives the hell it asked for.

At least, that is the way a good many theologians insist on describing the first third of the *Commedia*. And, of course, one wants to be convinced, especially if one has been bewitched by the beauty of Dante's verse and the majesty of his narrative gifts (particularly from the point of the encounter with the shade of Ulysses onward). I am not sure, however, that the text quite bears this picture out. For his part, at least, Dante gives no indication of seeing the matter this way at all. Once the poem has brought us into the "sorrowful city" and we have begun the descent along the terraces of hell, down to the devil's prison of ice, what unfolds before us is an almost unbearable succession of cunningly exotic savageries. If the torments of the damned that the poem describes have any sort of moral logic about them whatsoever, it is of at once the most inflexibly mechanical and the most inventively sadistic kind: an iron law of cause and effect, quite impersonal in its exactitude, and yet one expressing itself in a gaudy pageant of ever more ingenious, ever more inventive, ever more theatrically grotesque mockery, all of it plainly bereft of the least element of mercy. So, yes, perhaps the various torments described in the poem are in some way self-induced; but they nevertheless reflect an especially vindictive kind of proportional logic, and are, by virtue of their eternity, infinitely disproportionate to any finite deed. By the *Inferno*'s end, then, the only creator in the poem for whom one feels any spontaneous natural admiration is Dante; for Dante's God, if one is more or less emotionally intact, one can feel only a kind of remote, vacuous loathing. And, frankly, neither the *Purgatorio* nor the *Paradiso* quite succeeds at erasing that impression.

God, of course, ought not to be measured by the moral imagination of even as great a poet as Dante—or, for that matter, by anyone else's. And it is important to recall that much depends on the narrative of fall and salvation that one presumes. Here too, in my early years, Eastern Christian tradition offered me some relief from my fear that the Christian story as a whole might ultimately turn out to be a grim absurdity. I learned fairly early on—from exposure to Eastern Christian sources, from an attention to the original Greek of the New Testament (thank God for a classical education), and from a few especially civilized Western Christian thinkers (such as the magnificent George MacDonald [1824–1905])—that many of what had become the standard soteriological models of Christian tradition in its later centuries, especially in the West, were products of profound misreadings of the language of Christian scripture, abetted by absolutely abysmal historical forgetfulness. It is hard to know how often one hears it said, for instance, that the gospels or Paul's epistles teach that, on the cross of Christ, God poured out his wrath on sin, or that the Son was discharging a debt humanity owed the Father, or that Christ's blood was shed as a price paid by the Son to the Father to secure our release from the burden of that debt. And, supposedly, this was all inevitable not simply on account of sins we have individually committed, but because we have inherited a guilt contracted by the first parents of the race (which, of course, must be a purely imputed guilt, since personal guilt is not logically heritable). All of us, we are told, have been born damnable in God's eyes, already condemned to hell, and justly so. And yet God, out of God's love, races to rescue (some of) us from God's wrath, because God would otherwise be technically obliged to visit that wrath upon us, if lovingly, on account of that ancient trespass that bound us helplessly and damnably to sin before we ever existed; at the same time, however, God also lovingly fails or declines to rescue many of us, because he lovingly grants us the capacity freely to love, even if he lovingly withholds the conditions that would allow us to recognize him as the proper object of our love . . . (and so on). In the end, somehow, justice is served, love is vindicated, God is good; of that we can be sure.

Happily, all of that is degrading nonsense—an absolute midden of misconceptions, fragments of scriptural language wrenched out of context, errors of translation, logical contradictions, and (I suspect) one or two emotional pathologies. It came as a great consolation to me when I was still very young to discover that, in the first three or four centuries of the Christian era, none of these notions had yet taken root, in either the East or the West, and that for the most part the Eastern Christian world had remained innocent of the worst of them up until the present day, and furthermore that the New Testament, read in light of the proper tradition, turned out to contain nothing remotely like them. It is true, of course, that for Paul the cross of Christ revealed the *law's* wrath upon sin, in that it was an eminently *legal* murder; but it certainly revealed nothing about the will of God toward his creatures enslaved to death, and was in no sense a ransom paid to the Father to avert his wrath against us. For the earliest Christians, the story of salvation was entirely one of rescue, all the way through: the epic of God descending into the depths of human estrangement to release his creatures from bondage to death, penetrating even into the heart of hades to set the captives free and recall his prodigal children and restore a broken creation. The sacrifice of Christ was not a "ransom" paid to the Father, but rather the "manumission fee" (λύτρον, *lytron*) given to purchase the release of slaves held in bondage in death's household. It was a delight to me to discover various reflections on the part of theologians of the early centuries regarding whether it was proper to say that this fee had been paid to the devil, or only to death, or to no one as such at all (in the way that someone who lays down his or her life for another has "paid the price," even if there is no particular recipient for the fee thus rendered); and it was an even greater delight to discover that none of these same theologians had even momentarily considered the bizarre idea that this fee was a price paid to the Father—the coin of some sublimely circular transaction wherein God buys off God in order to spare us God's displeasure (rather like a bank issuing itself credit to pay off a debt it owes itself, using a currency it has minted for the occasion and certified in its value wholly on the basis of the very credit it is issuing to itself).

Even those, like Athanasius of Alexandria (c. 297–373), who saw the death of Christ as being *also* a kind of expiatory penalty that God took upon himself in our place, still did not understand that death as a sacrifice offered to avert or appease the wrath of the Father; it was simply the discharge of a debt we owed to death for our estrangement from God, yielded over on our behalf when we lacked the resources to do it for ourselves, so that God could reclaim us for himself without injustice. For the earliest and greatest of the church fathers in general, the story of salvation was really quite uncomplicated: We were born in bondage, in the house of a cruel master to whom we had been sold as slaves before we could choose for ourselves; we were born, moreover, not guilty or damnable in God's eyes, but nonetheless corrupted and enchained by mortality, and so destined to sin through a congenital debility of will; we were ill, impaired, lost, dying; we were in hell already.

But then Christ came to set us free, to buy us out of slavery, to heal us, to restore us to our true estate. In pursuit of those he loved, he invaded even the very depths of that hell we have made for ourselves and one another—in the cosmos, in history, in our own hearts—so as to *drag* us to himself (to use the actual language of John 12:32). Whatever variations were worked upon this grand, guiding theme in the early centuries of the faith, none of them ever incorporated the discordant claim that innocent blood had to be spilled to assuage God's indignation. And so, considered in these heartening terms, the language of hell seemed much less inexplicable to me, much less atrocious. If hell is simply God's enemy, which he has set out to conquer and to despoil of its captives, and if we then refuse to be joined to him in love and faith, and if we thereby condemn ourselves to a suffering that he does not desire for us, who can reproach God for our perversity?

As it happens, I do believe that the only hell that could possibly exist is the one of which those Christian contemplatives speak: the hatred within each of us that turns the love of others—of God and neighbor—into torment. It is entirely a state we impose upon ourselves. And the only Christian narrative of salvation that to me seems coherent is the one that the earliest church derived so directly from scripture: a relentless tale of rescue, conducted by a God who requires no tribute to win his forgiveness or love. Any other version of the story I regard not only as an exegetical and conceptual error (though certainly that), but also as a rather sickly parody of the Christianity of the New Testament. And yet, even this is not enough. Having come to this point, I find we have still merely arrived again where we began; our two questions remain as yet unanswered. Could such a refusal of God's love be sustained eternally while still being truly free? And would God truly be the

Good in an ultimate sense—and his act of creation good in a final sense—if the eternal loss of any soul to endless sorrow were a real possibility?

It seems clear to me that the only possible sensible answer to either question (not to belabor the issue) is an unambiguous no.

III

I am of a fairly argumentative disposition, it would be fair to say, but in this case I honestly have no desire to provoke a dispute, or even to inaugurate an animated discussion. It is not that I fear offending against pious belief, or that I suffer from any doubts regarding my views; rather, it is that I think most rhetorical engagements on these issues are largely pointless, partly because they are interminably repetitive, but mostly because they have less to do with genuine logical disagreement than with the dogmatic imperatives to which certain of the disputants feel bound. I am convinced that practically no one who holds firmly to the majority tradition regarding the doctrine of hell ultimately does so for any reason other than an obstinate, if largely unconscious, resolve to do so, prompted by the unshakable conviction that faith absolutely requires it. There are, I admit—unfortunately, I have met some of them—those Christians who are earnestly attached to the idea of an eternal hell not just because they feel they must be, but also because it is what they want to believe. For some of them, in fact, it is practically the best part of the story. It gives them a sense of belonging to a very small and select company, a very special club, and they positively relish the prospect of a whole eternity in which to enjoy the impotent envy of all those writhing, resentful souls that have been permanently consigned to an inferior neighborhood outside the gates. That is the sort of prestige that cannot be bought where the common people shop. In my experience, these kinds of believers can often be found among converts from one version of the faith to what they take to be an older, purer version—say, former Evangelicals who have embraced an especially severe form of traditionalist Catholicism or an especially fideistic kind of Eastern Orthodoxy or an especially siccative brand of orthodox Calvinism. I cannot help but see them as victims of their own diseased emotional conditions; and I have no doubt that, if one were to inquire deeply into their pasts, one would encounter any number of depressingly mundane psychological explanations for their heartlessness. Whatever the case, however, I refuse to believe that they are a particularly numerous or representative faction among believers. I still insist that most putative believers in an eternal hell do not really believe in it at all, but rather merely believe in their belief in it.

This is not to say, once more, that I want to impugn anyone's sincerity. Again, I take all parties at their words. I am quite sure, for instance, that a certain kind of soberly orthodox Christian thinker with which I am very familiar—say, a Catholic philosopher at a fine university, a devoted husband and father of five children—fervently believes that he believes the dominant doctrine of hell, and can provide very forceful and seemingly cogent arguments in its defense; I simply think he is deceiving himself. Then again, I may be the one who is deceived. My own, probably shameful prejudice—at least, most of the time—is that the whole question of hell is one whose answer should be immediately obvious to a properly functioning moral intelligence, and that a person either grasps the truth of the matter without much need to be persuaded by arguments (whether dialectically solvent or merely intuitive)

or does not: in the former case, that person will probably find
the way toward the correct view of the matter sooner or later,
even if he or she never fully formulates it, not even to himself
or herself; in the latter, that person probably lacks a certain capacity for seeing or acknowledging the obvious, and so will remain immune to even the most powerful case to the contrary.
But, putting the issue of my prejudice aside, I cannot take the
claims of this Catholic philosopher entirely seriously from any
angle, for the simple reason that his actions so resplendently
belie what he professes to believe. If he truly thought that our
situation in this world were as horribly perilous as he claims,
and that every mortal soul labored under the shadow of so
dreadful a doom, and that the stakes were so high and the odds
so poor for everyone—a mere three score and ten years to get
it right if we are fortunate, and then an eternity of agony in
which to rue the consequences if we get it wrong—he would
never dare to bring a child into this world, let alone five children; nor would he be able to rest even for a moment, because
he would be driven ceaselessly around the world in a desperate
frenzy of evangelism, seeking to save as many souls from the
eternal fire as possible. I think of him as a remarkably compassionate person, you see, and so his more or less sedentary and
distractedly scholarly style of life to my mind speaks volumes,
even libraries. If he were really absolutely convinced of the
things he thinks he is convinced of, but still continued to go
his merry recreant's way along the path of happy fatherhood
and professional contentment, he would have to be a moral
monster. But I do not think that he is a monster. So I have to
think instead that, in his heart of hearts, at a level of calm conviction so deeply hidden beneath veils of childhood indoctri-
nation that he is all but unaware of its existence, he keeps and
treasures the certainty that in the end—in the words of Dame

Julian of Norwich (1342–1416) — "All shall be well, and all manner of thing shall be well." And I believe that at that same level he also knows that nothing can be ultimately *well* if the happy final state of things for any of us has been purchased at the cost — or even only at the risk — of anyone else's eternal misery.

These, however, are matters to be dealt with below. I can take leave of them for now. Here I will simply note that there are plenty of vigorous and intelligent defenders of the received story who would indignantly reject these characterizations, and would rebuke me for presuming to know what they really believe better than they themselves do. And, in fact, I do admit it: it *is* presumptuous of me. I am taking their actions as indications of how I should interpret their words, and I am doing so because I have made certain assumptions about the deepest moral promptings of their souls. Perhaps I am getting things backward. Perhaps, instead of reading the complacency of certain Christians as a sign of their secret belief in the eventual rescue of all persons from death and misery, I should learn instead to interpret their inaction as an indication that those deep moral promptings do not actually exist. Perhaps what I should really conclude is that most of those who believe they believe in an eternal hell really do believe in it after all, at the very core of their beings, but are simply too morally indolent to care about anyone other than themselves and perhaps their immediate families. It seems to me, I have to say, that a person in that condition has probably already lost the heaven of which he or she feels so assured, but I suppose that that is not for me to say. Whatever the case, it may be that a sensitive conscience is not quite so liberally distributed a capacity as we like to imagine it is. Very well, then; if it is so, then it is so. But I still cannot grant the coherence of belief in a hell of eternal torment. Neither do I grant that anyone has ever succeeded in making an argument in favor of that belief that does not, once the mists of dogmatic commitment have cleared, turn out to be so internally contradictory as ultimately to constitute evidence for the opposition.

Doubting the Answers

I

For me, the first problem is that I find myself entirely unable to discover an intelligible grammar within which to make sense of the proposition that something like a hell of eternal torment truly exists, or could exist. I simply do not know how to forge any sort of durable conceptual connections among the various principal terms that have to be not merely juxtaposed, but ultimately reconciled with one another, in order to construct the standard infernalist arguments: "justice," "hell," "love," "freedom," "eternity," and so on. A sound definition of any of these words, it seems clear to me, including any adequate appreciation of the inevitable logical ramifications of that definition, will make it ever more difficult to integrate it into any kind of stable unity with all the other terms. The more any one of these words comes to be associated with a clear and distinct idea, the more subversive it becomes of the harmony of the whole. And, in this regard, no version of the standard arguments is conspicuously better than any other, as far as I can tell. As I have already noted, the most popular defense of the infernalist orthodoxy today is also, touchingly enough, the most tender-hearted: the argument, that is, from the rational freedom of the creature, and from the refusal of God to trespass upon that freedom, for fear of preventing the creature from achieving a true union of love with the divine (though, of course, unspeakable consequences await those who fail to do just this, which makes one wonder how neatly such an argument can discriminate between "pure" love and love motivated by fear). Over the years, I have encountered this take on the matter in a remarkable array of variations that are as a totality, even more remarkably, ultimately essentially identical with one another. All that really ever seems to change from one iteration to the next is the relative emphasis placed on one or another aspect of the argument's language, the method of exposition adopted, and the relative rhetorical gifts of the author. And this I find especially instructive, because there could scarcely be a worse defense of the idea of an eternal hell; it makes no sense whatsoever, no matter how appealing it seems on the surface. Yet there it is, repeated again and again with surprising frequency by a number of genuinely able Christian philosophers (and by a larger number of others who have at least a reputation for philosophical rigor).

I have only just finished reading, for instance, a recent restatement of the argument in a book by a venerable Catholic philosopher at a university with which I have an association; and I certainly made every effort I could to discover in its pages some new dimension of dialectical clarity that would make this entire line of reasoning seem more convincing to me. To no avail. All I ultimately found was a somewhat greater than usual reliance on the sentimental obscurantism that so often attaches to the word "love" when it is employed by theologians. Admittedly, it is a useful obscurantism; exploited to its fullest, it turns love into so imposingly mystifying and pliant a cipher that one can safely insert it into almost any gap in one's argument where an intelligible rationale or cogent motive has gone missing. In fact, used with sufficient suavity and dexterity, love can even serve, it turns out, as another name for what under normal circumstances would be called cruelty. But the effect is just so much verbal legerdemain at the end of the evening; should the spectators catch so much as a single glimpse of the hidden coin in the magician's hand or the elastic thread extending from his sleeve, the atmosphere of willingly suspended disbelief will dissipate immediately. In the case of this particular philosopher's book, the illusion consists in the combination of an essentially fantastic model of freedom—both as a rational capacity in the abstract and as an empirical possibility in the concrete—and an especially protean language of divine and human love, producing nothing more at the last than a warm enveloping fog of moral insensibility, through which the scandal of the traditional idea of hell is no longer visible. I should have expected nothing better. The reason that all versions of this argument are equally bad is a very simple one: Its logic is intrinsically defective, and nothing can be done to remedy its most essential flaws. But that is also what makes the argument's enduring popularity so significant. At least, I take it as compelling evidence that the infernalists' will to believe what they believe they must believe is so powerful that it can totally overwhelm reason in even the wisest of them.

It can even entail, when necessary, professing two antithetical principles at the same time, and simply refusing to see the contradiction. I shall not dwell here as long as I might on the proper definition of rational freedom, because the issue will recur below, in far greater detail; but I will allow myself to anticipate a few points. I have to say, if nothing else, that I have often been amazed by certain Thomists of my acquaintance who are committed to what is often called an "intellectualist" model of human liberty (as I am myself), but who also insist that it is possible for a soul freely to reject God's love, with such perfect perspicuity of understanding and intention as to merit eternal suffering. This is an altogether dizzying contradiction. In simple terms, that is to say, they want to assert that all true freedom is an orientation of the rational will toward an end that the mind takes in some sense to be the Good, and so takes also as the one end that can fulfill the mind's nature and supply its desires. This means that the better the rational will knows the Good for what it is—the more, that is, that the will is freed from those forces that distort reason and lead the soul toward improper ends—the more it will long for and seek after the true Good in itself; and, conversely, the more rationally it seeks the Good, the freer it is. In the terms of the great Maximus the Confessor (c. 580–662), the "natural will" within us, which is the rational ground of our whole power of volition, must tend only toward God as its true end, for God is goodness as such, whereas our "gnomic" or "deliberative" will can stray from him, but only to the degree that it has been blinded to the truth of who he is and what we are, and as a result has come to seek a false end *as* its true end. This means also that the rational soul cannot really will the evil as truly evil in an absolute sense, even if it knows that what it wills is formally regarded as wicked by normal standards. Such a soul must at the very least, even if it has lost the will to pursue goodness as a moral end, nevertheless seek what it takes to be good *for it*, however mistaken it may be in this judgment. In short, sin requires some degree of ignorance, and ignorance is by definition a diverting of the mind and will to an end they would not naturally pursue.

So far, so good. I agree with all of that, as I explain in my Fourth Meditation below. But then, secondly, these same

Thomists must say also that any rational will that ends its pere-
grinations in an eternal hell has found its way there by freely
rejecting God as the Good, and by seeking another good in
his place, knowing full well (or sufficiently well, at least) what
it was doing, and so justly inviting God's final condemnation
upon itself. To deny the former claim, after all, would be to
deny that God is himself the transcendent Good who is the
true ultimate object of rational love, and who is in fact himself
that transcendent horizon of all rational desire that permits
love to fix upon any finite objects as well. But to deny the latter
would be to deny that God is wholly just in his dealings with
his creatures. And so they simply affirm both propositions,
even though each contradicts the other. I cannot make the least
sense of this, I have to say. As far as I can see, something like a
transient and wavering balance can perhaps be struck between
the two claims, but only insofar as each side of the equation is
weighed against the other as its opposite—its counterweight,
so to speak—and therefore in purely relative degrees; and this,
of course, can yield only the certainty that the relation between
the soul's transgressions and the punishments they might elicit
must ultimately be a just proportion between two intrinsically
finite and qualified realities. It takes an almost heroic suspen-
sion of moral intelligence, it seems to me, to think instead that
this picture permits us to believe that any soul could possibly,
under the inevitable conditions of existence in this world, earn
for itself a penalty that is at once both "eternal" and "just." It
requires, at the very least, an almost total failure of imagination—by which I mean, principally, a failure to think through
what the word "eternal" actually means.

    I am not saying that we do not, in some very significant
sense, make our own exceedingly substantial voluntary con-
tributions to our estrangement from the Good in this life. No

doubt it is true that, as Moses Maimonides once observed, we
are what we have made ourselves, and no one drags us down
the path toward either compassion or cruelty, honesty or guile.
But precisely *how* true? Up to a certain point, it is undeniable; but, past that point, it is a manifest falsehood. There is
no such thing as perfect freedom in this life, or perfect understanding, and it is sheer nonsense to suggest that we possess
limitless or unqualified liberty. Therefore we are incapable of
contracting a limitless or unqualified guilt. There are always
extenuating circumstances. It might be pleasant (or might not
be) to imagine that Hitler was so entirely unlike the rest of
us that he was able, while enjoying both perfect sanity and an
unclouded knowledge of the truth, to elect freely to become
just as unimaginably evil as he was, in both his intentions and
his deeds. If nothing else, it might please us to think that we,
no matter what the circumstances and forces that formed us,
would never be capable of any evil remotely as enormous. I
certainly hope that this last is true; but we should not take too
much comfort in the thought even so. There are only two possibilities here, and neither delivers us from our dilemma: either
Hitler could, if he had been raised differently and exposed to
different influences in his youth, have turned out differently;
or he was congenitally wicked, and so from the moment of his
conception was irresistibly compelled along the path to his full
development as the *Führer,* so long as no countervailing circumstances prevented him from reaching his goal. But then, in
either case, his guilt was a qualified one: In the former, he was
at least partly the victim of circumstance; in the latter, he was
at least as much the victim of fate. In neither case was he ever
wholly free. These considerations do not excuse him, of course,
or make punishment for his evils unjust; he was himself in
any event, and the self that he was certainly merited damna-

tion. They do, however, oblige us to acknowledge that he was finite, and so could never have been capable of more than what finitude allows. Prometheus may have been able to provoke the tireless wrath of Zeus, but only because he was, after all, a titan, while his tormenter was merely a god: two very formidable but still limited beings, distinguished from one another only by differing degrees of finite power. Hitler, by contrast, was only human, and scarcely even that, while his final judge will presumably be the God of infinite goodness and infinite might; the disproportion between them is that of creature and creator, and so the difference in their relative powers, being infinite, dictates that a properly proportional justice for the former cannot exceed the scope of the moral capacities with which he has been endowed by the latter.

It can be painful—sometimes abhorrent—to us to admit this, but the character of even the very worst among us is in part the product of external contingencies, and somewhere in the history of every soul there are moments when a better way was missed by mischance, or by malign interventions from without, or by disorders of the mind within, rather than by any intentional perversity on the soul's own part. So no one could ever fulfill the criteria necessary justly to damn himself or herself to perpetual misery. Not even angels would have the power to condemn themselves to a condign eternity of suffering; as rational beings, they could never turn away from God entirely if they were not subject to *some* misapprehension regarding the Good in itself and their true relation to it, inasmuch as only the Good could ever really have the power to fulfill and satisfy their spiritual natures (though, admittedly, the dominant mediaeval theology of angels, which differed markedly from that of the early Christians, did occasionally make the entirely incoherent claim that the fallen angels had done just this). Even if a sinner's deeds were infinitely evil in every objective sense, as Hitler's were—utterly devoid, that is, of any residual quality of rational goodness—still the intentionality of a finite will, aboriginally prompted into action by a hunger for the Good, could never in perfect clarity of mind match the sheer nihilistic scope of the evil it perpetrates. Nor could any rational will that has ever enjoyed full freedom—which means a full rational awareness both of its own nature and of the nature of the Good as such—resist the love of God willfully for eternity. (But, again, this will be addressed below.)

Here, though, I have to note that it is a thoroughly modern and wholly illogical notion that the power of absolutely unpremised liberty, obeying no rationale except its own spontaneous volition toward whatever end it might pose for itself, is either a real logical possibility or, in any meaningful sense, a proper definition of freedom. An act of pure spontaneity on the part of a rational being, if such a thing were possible, would also be a pure brute event, without teleology or rational terminus, rather like a natural catastrophe. The will in such an eventuality would be nothing but a sort of spasmodic ebullition, emptily lurching toward—or, really, just lurching aimlessly in the direction of—one chance object or another, without any true purpose. A choice made without rationale is a contradiction in terms. At the same time, any movement of the will prompted by an *entirely* perverse rationale would be, by definition, wholly irrational—insane, that is to say—and therefore no more truly free than a psychotic episode. The more one is in one's right mind—the more, that is, that one is conscious of God as the Goodness that fulfills all beings, and the more one recognizes that one's own nature can have its true completion and joy nowhere but in him, and the more one is unfettered by distorting misperceptions, deranged passions, and the encumbrances of past mistakes—the more inevitable is one's surrender to God. Liberated from *all* ignorance, emancipated from *all* the adverse conditions of this life, the rational soul could freely will only its own union with God, and thereby its own supreme beatitude. We are, as it were, doomed to happiness, so long as our natures follow their healthiest impulses unhindered; we cannot *not* will the satisfaction of our beings in our true final end, a transcendent Good lying behind and beyond all the proximate ends we might be moved to pursue. This is no constraint upon the freedom of the will, coherently conceived; it is simply the consequence of possessing a nature produced by and for the transcendent Good: a nature whose proper end has been fashioned in harmony with a supernatural purpose. God has made us for himself, as Augustine would say, and our hearts are restless till they rest in him. A rational nature seeks a rational end: Truth, which is God himself. The irresistibility of God for any soul that has truly been set free is no more a constraint placed upon its liberty than is the irresistible attraction of a flowing spring of fresh water in a desert place to a man who is dying of thirst; to choose not to drink in that circumstance would be not an act of freedom on his part, but only a manifestation of the delusions that enslave him and force him to inflict violence upon himself, contrary to his nature. A woman who chooses to run into a burning building not to save another's life, but only because she can imagine no greater joy than burning to death, may be exercising a kind of "liberty," but in the end she is captive to a far profounder poverty of rational freedom.

So, yes, we can act irrationally, but that is no more than a trivial deliberative power; it is not yet true liberty. Only because there is such a thing as a real rational terminus for intentional action, which is objectively distinguishable from ir-

rational ends, is there such a thing as real freedom. This is, in
fact, an ancient Christian orthodoxy, common to the teachings
of the church fathers and great mediaeval theologians; and,
were it not true, the whole edifice of the Christian conception
of existence and of creation and of God and of the unity of
the ontological and moral dimensions of reality would entirely
collapse. Even the suicide is merely fleeing pain and seeking a
peace that the world cannot give, though he or she might be
able in the crucial moment of decision to imagine this peace
only under the illusory form of oblivion; his or her fault is one
only of perception, in a moment of severe confusion and sad-
ness, and certainly not some ultimate rejection of God. One
cannot even choose nothingness, at least not *as* nothingness;
to will nonexistence positively, one must first conceive it as a
positive end, and so one can at most choose it as the "good"
cessation of this world, and therefore as just another mask of
that which is supremely desirable in itself. In the end, even
when we reject the good, we always do so out of a longing for
the Good. We may not explicitly conceive of our actions in this
way, but there is no question that this is what we are doing.
We act always toward an end that we desire, whether morally,
affectively, or pathologically; and, so long as we are rational
agents, that end is the place where the "good" and the "desirable" are essentially synonymous terms. And our ability to will
anything at all, in its deepest wellsprings, is sustained by this
aboriginal orientation within us toward that one transcendental Good that alone can complete us, and that prompts reason
to move the will toward an object of longing. Needless to say,
we can induce moral ignorance in ourselves through our own
wicked actions and motives; but, conversely, those wicked actions and motives are themselves possible only on account of
some degree of prior ignorance on our part. This circle admits

of no breaks; it has no beginning or end, no point of entry or exit. When, therefore, we try to account for the human rejection of God, we can never trace the wanderings of the will back to some primordial moment of perfect liberty, some epistemically pristine instant when a perverse impulse spontaneously arose within an isolated, wholly sane individual will, or within a mind perfectly cognizant of the whole truth of things; we will never find that place where some purely uncompelled apostasy on the part of a particular soul, possessed of a perfect rational knowledge of reality, severed us from God. Such a movement of volition would have had no object to prompt it, and so could never have been a real rational choice. Thus it is, for instance, that the Eastern church fathers, when interpreting the story of Eden, generally tended to ascribe the cause of the fall to the childlike ignorance of unformed souls, not yet mature enough to resist false notions (and this, lest we forget, accords exactly with the Eden story in Genesis, which tells the story of two persons so guileless and ignorant that they did not even know they were naked until a talking snake had shown them the way to the fruit of knowledge). Hence, absolute culpability—*eternal* culpability—lies forever beyond the capacities of any finite being. So does an eternal *free* defiance of the Good. We are not blameless, certainly; but, then again, that very fact proves that we have never been entirely free not to be blameless—and so neither can we ever be entirely to blame.

II

None of this should need saying, to be honest. We should all already know that whenever the terms "justice" and "eternal punishment" are set side by side as if they were logically compatible, the boundaries of the rational have been violated. If we were not so stupefied by the hoary and venerable myth that eternal damnation is an essential element of the original Christian message (which, not to spoil later plot developments here, it is not), we would not even waste our time on so preposterous a conjunction. From the perspective of Christian belief, the very notion of a punishment that is not intended ultimately to be remedial is morally dubious (and, I submit, anyone who doubts this has never understood Christian teaching at all); but, even if one believes that Christianity makes room for the condign imposition of purely retributive punishments, it remains the case that a retribution consisting in unending suffering, imposed as recompense for the actions of a finite intellect and will, must be by any sound definition disproportionate, unjust, and at the last nothing more than an expression of sheer pointless cruelty. Again, it should be enough to make ourselves reflect seriously upon what the word "eternity" actually means. Moreover, given that—as I have just argued—no rejection of God on the part of the rational soul is possible apart from some quantum of ignorance and misapprehension and personal damage, we would certainly expect divine justice to express itself in a punishment that is properly educative, and therefore conducive of moral reform. A number of Christian thinkers down the centuries have been sufficiently aware of this, and of the impossibility of striking a plausible balance between finite sin and infinite misery (since the imbalance is, after all, soberly calculated, an infinite one), that they have felt moved to explain the problem away by any number of cunning or desperate devices. The most august of these is the claim that the guilt for any crime must be measured not by the intention of the criminal, but solely by the dignity of the one offended against; and this supposedly explains things adequately, because God is infinite, and infinitely good, and infinitely worthy of obedience and love, and so . . . well, you can fill in the rest. Then again, why bother? It is nonsense, after all. As before, we are confronted by a claim that no one would seriously entertain for a moment if not for the emotional pressure exerted by the conviction that he or she *must* believe in an eternal hell that is somehow the work of love and justice, rather than of malice. Any logical definition of penal justice requires a due proportion between (in forensic terms) a *mens rea* and the *actus reus*—between, on the one hand, the intentions, knowledge, and powers of the malefactor and, on the other, the objective wickedness of the transgression. Otherwise the very concept of justice has been rendered entirely vacuous. But, of course, absolutely no one could really then fulfill the requirements of a justice that eventuates in eternal damnation, because no one could actually achieve perfect culpability; therefore, such justice is no justice at all.

Another, even feebler attempt to make sense of eternal retribution is the traditional claim that a soul cannot alter its orientation after death. Sometimes this curious constraint is presented as a simple fiat of the divine will: These, it seems, are merely the inabrogable rules of the contest God has devised for us, which make the stakes of our brief sojourn here on earth so immense—so infinite, in fact. I am not sure quite what the appeal of that argument is meant to be. Left to itself, it makes the disproportion between the culpability of which we are capable and the verdict to which we are subject all the more grotesque in its arbitrariness. Everything has been reduced to a matter of luck, and then only for the sake of a kind of game. Really, though, this is just one more entirely willful claim, adduced on the fly to make the senseless seem sensible; and frankly, if it were true, it would make existence itself the cruelest imaginable misfortune, visited on us by a heartlessly capricious gamester. At other times, however, this alleged postmortem inalterability of the will is explained in terms of some hazy metaphysics of the conditions of disembodied spirits. Supposedly—so, at least, argue a few Thomist philosophers of my acquaintance—the soul detached from its carnal frame is no longer mutable, and so no longer able to change its course. Obviously, that too is just a blank assertion, since any finite rational nature can change the intentions of its will, even if its physical substance is fixed; how else—presuming, that is, an orthodoxy that Thomism positively insists upon— could bodiless intelligences like angels have ever fallen? And then, of course, there is that matter of resurrection, which any good Catholic also confesses as a sure promise of the faith. According to my acquaintances, the reason that this latter makes no difference is that the interval of disembodied existence between death and resurrection freezes the soul in its final state, and the risen body, being immune to generation or decay, no longer possesses a changeable nature. Precisely why this last claim would be of any significance for the powers of the risen creature's rational will is not clear to me, nor have any of my acquaintances quite succeeded in explaining it to me in a way that does not seem to confuse physical and spiritual categories, or material causality and mental intentionality. As contradictions go, that one is, if nothing else, amusingly sharp. It would be a very odd Thomist, after all, who believed that mental intentionality emerges from wholly physical states, since such a notion runs contrary to the whole of Thomist metaphysics; so it seems odd for any to suggest that physical immutability should equate to moral inalterability.

    I do not blame my acquaintances for these obscurities, however. The only reason for their inability to make the argument clear is that the argument itself happens to be intrinsically nonsensical; it is a claim made in desperation only because no better, more plausible claim was available. So, really, what can my Thomist acquaintances do in the end other than repeat their asseveration, as though reciting their catechism, and to do so repeatedly until they have convinced themselves that it really does all make some sort of sense after all? Even the most rigorous reasoning, however, if based on absurd premises, can yield at best only gibberish, at worst cynical sophistries. And, really, none of this matters much in the end. Once more, not a single one of these attempted justifications for the idea of an eternal hell actually improves the picture of God with which the infernalist orthodoxy presents us, and it is this that should be the chief concern of any believer. All of these arguments still oblige one to believe that a benevolent and omnipotent God would willfully create rational beings destined for an endless torment that they could never, in any rational calculus of personal responsibility, earn for themselves; and to believe also that this, somehow, is essential to the good news Christianity brought into the world.

In the end, there really is only one logical terminus toward which all these lines of reasoning can lead: When all the possible paths of evasion have tapered away among the weeds, one has to stop, turn around, retrace one's steps back to the beginning of the journey, and finally admit that, if there really is an eternal hell for finite spirits, then it has to be the case that God condemns the damned to endless misery not on account of any sane proportion between what they are capable of meriting and how he chooses to requite them for their sins, but solely as a demonstration of his power to do as he wishes. Hence, for instance, classical Thomism, at least in the "manualist" tradition that so dominated the reading of Aquinas from the sixteenth century through the early twentieth, was

as purely double-predestinarian as just about any school of
Reformed tradition ever succeeded in being: All souls come
into this world already ineluctably destined by divine decree
for eternal bliss or eternal torment, and in either case not in
respect of any divine favor they could ever have merited on
their own, but solely as a revelation of the full range of God's
power and majesty. Admittedly, Thomists of that persuasion
have not generally chosen to speak of this as a strictly *double*
predestination, in the way a Calvinist might; they have preferred instead to make a specious distinction between, on the
one hand, God's irresistible predestination of the elect to beatitude and, on the other, the "irresistible permissive decrees" by
which he sends the derelict to a damnation they never had the
power to escape. But that need detain no one (for any number
of obvious reasons, moral and logical, as well as any number
of other more philosophically abstruse reasons, none of which
should occupy our attention at this point). Far preferable, I
would think, is the less convoluted and more ingenuous language of predestination that one finds in Reformed tradition,
and in the theology of John Calvin (1509–1564) in particular.
There, if nothing else, one encounters perfect candor. Calvin
draws no meaningless distinctions between the way God acts
in predestining the elect to salvation and the way he acts in
predestining the derelict to eternal agony. In Book III of his
Institutes (III.23.7, to be precise), he even asserts that God
predestined the human fall from grace, precisely because the
whole of everything—creation, fall, redemption, judgment,
the eternal bliss of heaven, the endless torments of hell, and
whatever else—exists solely for the sake of a perfect display
of the full range of God's omnipotent sovereignty (which for
some reason absolutely must be displayed).

     It is hard for me to know exactly how to respond to this

vision of Christianity, I have to say. In part, this is because I know it to be based on a notoriously confused reading of scripture, one whose history goes all the way back to the late Augustine—a towering genius whose inability to read Greek and consequent reliance on defective Latin translations turned out to be the single most tragically consequential case of linguistic incompetence in Christian history. In equal part, however, it is because I regard the picture of God thus produced to be a metaphysical absurdity: a God who is at once supposedly the source of all things, and yet also one whose nature is necessarily thoroughly polluted by arbitrariness (and, no matter how orthodox Calvinists might protest, there is no other way to understand the story of election and dereliction that Calvin tells), which would mean that in some sense he is a finite being, in whom possibility exceeds actuality and the irrational exceeds the rational. There is no need to dilate on that here, however; it touches upon technical philosophical issues that are not directly relevant to this book's topic, and I am not interested in pursuing the debate just now because, frankly, it is all of somewhat subordinate importance to me. Of far greater concern than either of these theological defects—either the deeply misguided scriptural exegesis or the inept metaphysics of the divine—is the moral horror in such language. In one sense, this is a quality I sometimes almost admire. True, the Calvinist account of predestination is unquestionably the most terrifying and severe expression of the late Augustinian heritage; but it is at least bracing in its consistency, in a way that other expressions of that tradition are not. Of course, that is also its principal vice; but there is no hint of duplicity in it. Calvin makes no effort to deceive either us or himself that there is some deeper kindness in the doctrine he proclaims, hidden from our sinful eyes only by our own depravity. He proclaims that God hates the damned, and in fact created them to be the objects of his hatred (see his commentaries on the epistles of John). For him, the true unadorned essence of the whole story is nothing more than sheer absolute power exercising itself for power's sake, which therefore necessarily manifests itself in boundless cruelty no less than in boundless generosity. Calvinists, of course, will object to my phrasing it that way; but it is accurate all the same.

Once again, though, I have to confess a certain admiration here; I can see a certain illuminating logic in this perspective, even when approaching the matter in purely human terms. Consider, for instance, the emperor Domitian, who according to the Roman historian Suetonius once invited one of his stewards to dine with him in his private apartments—to recline in his presence, to eat from his dishes, to share in delicacies normally reserved for only the most powerful man in the world and his cherished intimates. It was the highest honor the steward had ever received or could ever have hoped for; it was certainly nothing he would ever have imagined he had any right to expect. The next day, Domitian ordered that the steward be crucified. Now that is impressive, one has to say. It was as grand a demonstration of absolute sovereignty as one could ever imagine, and perfect proof of how immeasurably far above the level of the ordinary categories of good and evil such sovereignty operates. It showed with utter clarity that the gifts imparted by absolute power are entirely gracious, and that those upon whom they are bestowed have no right to presume them; and it proved just as emphatically that such power is, for this very reason, bound to no common measure of justice or mercy, and so properly reveals itself in the sheer capriciousness of its malice no less than in the lavishness of its largesse. It is an old adage of certain streams of Reformed thought that

God could have created us all for everlasting torment if he had so wished, and it would have been perfectly just for him to do so simply because it lay in his power. To me, this seems like the most decadent theology imaginable, and certainly blasphemous through and through. But I do not hold Calvin himself necessarily accountable for this, since in this matter he was the product of centuries of bad scriptural interpretation and even worse theological reasoning; he differed little from many of his contemporaries, Protestant and Catholic alike, except that (as I have said) his thinking exhibited a greater consistency than anyone else's. Nevertheless, to me the God of Calvinism at its worst (as in those notorious lines in Book III of the *Institutes*) is simply Domitian made omnipotent. If that were Christianity, it would be too psychologically diseased a creed to take seriously at all, and its adherents would deserve only a somewhat acerbic pity, not respect. If this is one's religion, then one is simply a diabolist who has gotten the names in the story confused. It is a vision of the faith whose scriptural and philosophical flaws are numerous and crucial, undoubtedly; but those pale in comparison to its far more disturbing moral hideousness. This aspect of orthodox Calvinism is for me unsurpassable evidence for my earlier claim that a mind conditioned to believe that it must believe something incredible is capable of convincing itself to accept just about anything, no matter how repellant to reason (or even good taste). And yet I still insist that, judging from the way Christians actually behave, no one with the exception of a few religious sociopaths really believes any of it as deeply as he or she imagines.

There is, moreover, probably a very profound truth hidden in the Calvinist version of the story of salvation and damnation, even if it is a truth that leads in quite a different direction from the one that Calvinist orthodoxy suggests. At least,

I agree with Reformed tradition that, for Christian thought in general, the question of one's just deserts before God is irrelevant—as it was, for instance, for the woman taken in adultery. If what the New Testament says about God is true, then it is God's will not to repay us according to our merits, but simply to claim for himself those of his creatures who had been lost in slavery to death. I remain convinced that no one, logically speaking, could merit eternal punishment; but I also accept the obverse claim that no one could merit grace. This does not mean, however, that grace must be rare in order to be truly gracious, as so many in the infernalist party so casually assume it must. Grace universally given is still grace. A gift made to everyone is no less a gift, and a gift that is intrinsically precious need not be rare to be an act of the highest generosity. Conversely, that gift becomes no more precious—indeed, it becomes much less so—if it is certified in its value by being distributed only parsimoniously. Our very existence is an unmerited gift, after all (unless, of course, there really is an eternal hell, in which case it is also, and perhaps preponderantly, an unmerited brutality). More to the point, if Paul is right, then—whereas natural justice is wholly concerned with matters of law and proportional consequences—the supernatural justice revealed in Christ consists in God's victory over all the powers that separate his creation from him, and to that degree is as "unjust" as any other act of wholly unmerited mercy is. So the entire question of deserts may be set aside for the moment, as well as any anxiety regarding a proper appreciation of divine grace, because the more basic and comprehensive issue remains that of the essential character of the God Christians think they believe in. The infernalist argument from creaturely freedom is a silly distraction at the end of the day. True, it presumes a model of freedom that is inherently absurd, as is well

worth pointing out, and it multiplies that absurdity by an infinite sum in claiming that this fabulous power of free choice
could ever eventuate in a rejection of God extending into eternity. But the far deeper problem with the infernalist orthodoxy,
as far as I am concerned, is the exceedingly obvious one that
the idea of an eternal hell, no matter what terms one uses to defend it, forces one to accept certain conclusions about God—
understood both as the free creator of the world and as the
only possible transcendental end of the natural rational will—
that ultimately render a vast number of traditional Christian
doctrines and moral claims totally empty. And, in fact, this
is where I begin in the meditations that follow: not from the
question of creaturely freedom, which can be deferred to the
end, but rather from that of divine goodness (which, it turns
out, is nowhere near so simple a matter as one might think).

III

Sometimes childish imagery—even childish anthropomorphisms—can have a certain convenient power for elucidating
things that should be clear already, but often are not. Take a
clear example: Christ instructs his followers to think of God
on the analogy of a human father, and to feel safe in assuming
that God's actions toward them will display something like—
but also something far greater than—paternal love. "Is it not
the case that no man among you, if his son should ask for a
loaf of bread, would give him a stone? Or, if he should also ask
for a fish, would give him a serpent? If you, therefore, who are
wicked, know to give good gifts to your children, how much
more will your Father in the heavens give good things to those
who ask him" (Matthew 7:9–11; cf. Luke 11:11–13). Moreover,
Ephesians 3:14–15 identifies God's as a universal fatherhood,

extending to all the children of the heavens and the earth. It is
perfectly reasonable, then, to allow this similitude a particularly privileged status when trying to think about God's relations to his creatures. But perhaps, in order to understand this
fully, we must almost force ourselves to reason in a childlike
way. We can then at the very least gain some sense of what *not*
to expect from God. For instance, a father who punishes his
child for any purpose other than that child's correction and
moral improvement, and who even then fails to do so only re-
luctantly, is a poor father. One who brutally beats his child, or
wantonly inflicts needless pain of any kind upon his child, is
a contemptible monster. And one who surrenders his child to
fate, even if that fate should consist in the entirely "just" consequences of his child's own choices and actions, is an altogether
unnatural father—not a father at all, really, except in the most
trivial biological sense. Natural justice—in fact, proportional
justice as such—is not the primary business of fathers. It is
their responsibility to continue to love their children in all conditions, to seek their children's well-being and (if need be) ref-
ormation, and to use whatever natural powers they possess to
save their children from ruin. (What a happy circumstance,
then, if a father happens to possess infinite power.) Paternal
love has nothing to do with proportion; its proper "measure"
is total, ceaseless abandon. This is something that indeed any
child should be able to grasp. Hence we should be able to grasp
it as well. For some reason, however, we usually are not.

    One of the more irksome complaints often raised against
any moral critique of the infernalist orthodoxies is that it involves judging the acts of God according to some ethical standard applicable to finite creatures, and thereby attempts to
trespass upon the inaccessible transcendence of the one who

creates all things for his own purposes. This simply is not so. For one thing, it is not God we are trying to judge when we voice our moral alarm at the idea of an eternal hell, but only the stories we are accustomed to telling about him. One does not have to imagine God to be some finite ethical agent, subject to moral truths outside himself, to note that the goodness traditionally attributed to the Christian God—indeed, that "Goodness-as-such" with which God's nature is said to be identical—must have some analogical index in the moral truths to which Christians are also supposedly bound. Some Christians, even some who accept the ancient metaphysical definitions of God as the Good in itself, often affect to obey so exaggerated an apophatic stricture on their reasoning with regard to God as to render all analogy impossible, and thus to reduce all theological statements to sheer assertions emanating from some mysterious source of authority that itself (again, because analogical thinking has been abandoned) cannot be certified by any power of reason at all. Faith thus becomes nothing but mindless submission to a collection of intrinsically unintelligible oracles arriving from an entirely hidden source. Now, admittedly, there is a "nominalist" and "voluntarist" tradition in some schools of Western Christian thought that, rather than assuming God's nature to be convertible with the transcendental perfections (goodness, truth, beauty, unity, being), imagines God as a kind of abyss of pure, pre-moral will, entirely hidden behind the veils of nature and history. But, for any number of scriptural and logical reasons, that way of seeing things has rightly been rejected by the majority tradition as doctrinally depraved and philosophically inane. Still, even Christians adhering to a more orthodox and rationally rigorous understanding of God sometimes find it all too convenient

to invoke "divine transcendence" or "divine incomprehensi-
bility" as a dissembling euphemism for the unresolved logical
contradictions in their own systems of belief.

   More than one captious critic of that lecture of mine
from 2015 that I mentioned above in my introduction cited
a book by the Dominican philosopher Brian Davies called
The Reality of God and the Problem of Evil (2006), and specifically the claim Davies repeatedly makes therein that God is
not an ethical agent, and so we cannot draw any conclusions
about how he should act toward his creatures in any particular
situation. Whether those who invoked the book were always
quite as cognizant of Davies's point as they thought they were
I will not bother to argue, one way or the other, since it is a
book toward which I have distinctly mixed feelings. I happen
to agree with most of the basic metaphysical principles that
Davies presumes or propounds, while disagreeing entirely
with a whole host of the conclusions he draws from them. On
this one issue, however, he is obviously correct: If God is God,
in any philosophically coherent sense of the word, then clearly
God is not, like one of us, an ethical agent. He is not a finite,
psychologically limited, individual rational being, navigating
successive moral situations, required to make deliberative ethical decisions in submission to some standard of goodness or to
some deontological code of immediate obligations that stands
higher in the scale of reality than himself. But so what? To be
honest, this is little other than a banal truism of metaphysical
reasoning. It is no more startling an insight, from the perspective of traditional Christian thought, than the equally undeniable assertion that God is not good in the way a finite being
might or might not be good, but is instead infinite Goodness
as such; or that he is not merely something true, but is rather
Truth in its transcendent fullness; or that he is not something

beautiful, but is instead absolute Beauty; or that he is not a discrete unified thing, but is rather the transcendent Unity in which all reality subsists; or that he is not a discrete being among other beings, but is himself infinite subsistent Being as such, whereon all things depend.

Far from constituting an obstacle to analogical statements about God, it is precisely this difference between the finite and the infinite, or between the immanent and the transcendent, that secures the rational basis of all such statements. Because God is infinitely transcendent of what we are, we cannot "univocally" predicate anything of him as we would predicate it of finite things; but, since he is himself the infinite fullness of those transcendental perfections in which creatures participate (as various modes and reflections of their divine source), neither are we limited to purely "equivocal" predications. It is not the case that the words we use have no continuity of meaning whatsoever between the senses with which they are applied to worldly things and the ways in which they point toward the transcendent mystery of God. So, yes, God is not a moral agent, but only because he is transcendent Moral Agency as such. That is to say, we are moral agents as a result of privation, because we are not in ourselves goodness in itself— goodness is not analytically convertible with our essence, that is to say—and so we have a necessarily synthetic relation to the transcendent Good. We can achieve some degree of goodness, and thereby participate more deeply in real being, or we can fail to do so and gravitate instead toward nothingness, moral and ontological. God is not like that, obviously. He is, according to Christian tradition, the Good as such. At the same time, Christian doctrine proclaims him to be a living God; he is himself an infinite intentionality toward the fullness of his own essence, the infinite procession of omnipotent and omni-

scient love toward the infinite benignity of his own nature, all
of whose acts terminate in perfect goodness. For Christians,
this is frequently stated in trinitarian terms: God loves his own
essence as known in his Logos and delights in it in his Spirit.
Thus, he is unlike finite moral agents precisely by being infinitely better than they—by being himself, that is, perfect benevolence, an infinite willing and loving of the Good, revealed
as such for Christians in Christ.

Hence, again, it really is only a spurious sort of apopha-
ticism that prompts a Christian at this point to refuse to draw
obvious conclusions from what Christian tradition claims are
revealed truths about God. And one principle that absolutely
must be deduced from Christian metaphysical tradition, and
from the logic of "classical theism" as a whole, is that it is *precisely because* God is not some finite ethical agent—precisely,
that is, because he is transcendent perfection and simplicity
rather than a mutable individual of variable goodness—that
one can assume that all his acts must be expressive of his nature's infinite benevolence. He is not, like one of us, a limited
and changeable thing among other limited changeable things,
who might on occasion act in ways contrary to his nature. To
imagine that he could ever possibly be only imperfectly and
inconstantly good in this fashion would be the worst kind of
anthropomorphism. It would reduce him to a finite instance
of reality, in whom the possible exceeds the actual. It would
make him a conditioned being, dependent for what he is on
a reality greater than himself: a goodness that he only partly
exemplifies. Or else—what amounts to the same thing—it
would reduce "goodness" itself to an artifact of the will of some
"supreme being" rather than one of the "divine names": one,
that is, of the true manifestations of the divine nature, convertible in reference with the very essence of God. If that were

how things were, then indeed we would be able to hold God accountable to ethical standards beyond himself. But this is logically impossible. (And here, for anyone uncertain about the logic of the traditional Christian metaphysical claims regarding God, I refer readers to my earlier book *The Experience of God*.) So, really, it makes no sense to take a metaphysical principle as trivially true as "God is not an ethical agent" as a prohibition upon all moral interrogations of Christian teachings about God. In point of fact, a moral agent is able to fail to act justly precisely because he or she suffers the limitation of possessing goodness only by appropriation; he or she is good only so long as he or she willingly acts in conformity with Moral Agency as such. That infinite Moral Agency itself, however, suffers from no defect in respect of its own nature, and so is never unjust. So, if the traditional Christian philosophical claims about God are true, we are permitted to arrive at all sorts of analogical conclusions regarding how God might act, so long as our frame of reference is correct. If we know what it is for an ethical agent to act in accord with moral goodness, then we have some sense, however limited, of what moral goodness is in itself, in God who is its source and substance.

Now, obviously, this still does not mean — Davies is absolutely right about this — that we have any warrant for trying to pass judgment on what we take to be God's actions in any particular isolated worldly event, since any such event is one whose causes and consequences and conditions and circumstances all quickly slip beyond our ken, and we can have no sense of how that event fits into the pattern of the whole of things. Any such judgment on our part would be made from an infinitely inadequate perspective. If, however, we are not confronted just by this or that particular contingent tragic or terrible episode or circumstance, of which we are trying to make sense within the context of all other contingent events and conditions, but are instead presented with a comprehensive story that purports to be nothing less than the total narrative and total rationale of all God's actions in creation, then we may indeed pass judgment on that story's plausibility. In fact, it is morally required of us to do so; not to judge is a dereliction of our rational vocation to know and affirm the Good. And here, recall again, we are not assessing God's acts against some higher standard of ethical action; we are merely measuring the stories we tell about him against his own supposed revealed nature as the transcendent Good. It is our story that is being judged for its internal coherence, in keeping with our rational grasp of justice and benevolence, not God who is being judged according to some external scale of ethical values. Thus, for instance, it is perfectly permissible to say with confidence that God, by his nature, could not create a reality containing rational creatures, all of whom, for no reason save the exercise of the divine will, he keeps entirely ignorant of the Good during their lives, and then mercilessly consigns to eternal torment thereafter as a penalty for their misdeeds. Because he is the Good itself, God cannot be the author of absolute injustice, absolute evil; such an irrational possibility would be a limitation upon the infinite freedom with which he expresses his nature.

In fact, if God were some impulsively erratic or playfully mercurial psychological personality, capable of occasionally contradicting his own essence just to make the point that he can, all theological language would be just so much meaningless babble. And, if God's essence were nothing more than sheer indeterminate will, detached from the measure of the Good, he would be both a logical contradiction in himself, and an utterly impenetrable enigma or ultimate absurdity in regard to us. So it is no error of reason for a believer to refuse to assent to a supposedly complete narrative of God and creation if that narrative severs every analogical connection between goodness among creatures and the goodness of God. In fact, reason and faith alike forbid such assent; to believe solely because one thinks faith demands it, in despite of all the counsels of reason, is actually a form of disbelief, of faithlessness. Submission to a morally unintelligible narrative of God's dealings with his creatures would be a kind of epistemic nihilism, reducing the act of fidelity to God to a brutishly obstinate infidelity to reason (whose substance, again, is God himself). Submission of that kind could not be sincere, because it would make "true faith" and "bad faith"—devotion to truth and betrayal of truth—one and the same thing. So we can in fact know that, for instance, the unsavory assertions made about God in Book III of the *Institutes* are false, not because God is an ethical agent, but precisely because he is not. We know that, logically speaking, he is not merely obliged to do good things; rather, he is himself transcendent goodness, and so cannot be the source of injustice. He does not flit capriciously between isolated expressions of his true nature and isolated departures from it. He is the ground and substance and end of every moral action. And, as we have some very real knowledge of what moral action is, we know something also of who God therefore is. So we should really stop telling such sordid lies about him.

IV

There is little more that needs to be said at this point. I have posed the questions that I have always found the most troubling with regard to talk of hell, and I have rejected the answers typically advanced against the doubts I have raised. So now I want to try to think through what the idea of an eternal hell really means, once one has stripped away all the traditional facile justifications and beguiling rhetoric and pious dogmatisms. What remains when one has done that, I believe, is something quite ridiculous, and quite abominable. For what it is worth, however, I do in fact believe in hell, though only in the sense of a profound and imprisoning misery that we impose upon ourselves by rejecting the love that alone can set us free. I believe, in fact, that I have on occasion experienced that hell from within its walls, so to speak; I suspect that most of us, at least past a certain age, have done so. And it is a captivity from which we would be foolish to imagine we can free ourselves on our own. Practically all of us go through life as prisoners of our own egos, which are no more than the shadows cast by our souls, but which are nonetheless quite impossible for us to defeat without assistance and without grace. Hence, a secret that we all too often hide from ourselves is that we walk in hell every day. There is, though, another and greater secret too: We also walk in heaven, also every day. This too we can occasionally see, though usually only in rare moments of spiritual wakefulness or imaginative transport. Redemption, then, if there is such a thing, must consist ultimately in a conversion of the heart so complete that one comes to see heaven for what it is—and thus also comes to see, precisely where one formerly had perceived only the fires of hell, the transfiguring glory of infinite love. And "love never fails" (1 Corinthians 13:8).

II
Apokatastasis

FOUR MEDITATIONS

It is not the way of the compassionate Maker to create rational beings in order to deliver them over mercilessly to unending affliction in punishment for things of which He knew even before they were fashioned, aware how they would turn out when He created them—and whom nonetheless He created.

—ST. ISAAC OF NINEVEH, *ASCETICAL HOMILIES*

First Meditation

Who Is God?

The Moral Meaning of Creatio ex Nihilo

I

Let me start again, in a more purely reflective vein. And let me start also by admitting that I have always—or, at least, for as long as I can remember thinking about such things—been an instinctive universalist as regards the question of the ultimate destiny of souls. Part of the reason for this, I confess, is purely affective: I have always found what became the traditional majority Christian view of hell—that is, a conscious state of perpetual torment—a genuinely odious idea, both morally and emotionally, and still think it the single best argument for doubting the plausibility of the Christian faith as a coherent body of doctrine or as a morally worthy system of devotion. But my inclinations in this direction have also—at least, as long as I have had any formal interest in theology— been encouraged by a number of considerations regarding certain traditional Christian beliefs about the nature of God's act in Christ, the moral character of God, the proper interpretation of the eschatological language of scripture, the nature of spiritual personality, and so on. And, I should note, I fell early under the influence of certain figures from the first several centuries of the church who seemed to me to possess an especially sane understanding of the "good tidings": Origen, Gregory of Nyssa, Isaac of Nineveh, and a number of other explicit universalists, as well as Maximus the Confessor, who never openly professed universalism but whose entire system of theology seems to me to leave no room for any other conclusion (not that I have any desire to enter into that debate here). Before addressing any of these issues or figures, however, I want to make it absolutely clear that I approach these meditations not as a seeker tentatively and timidly groping his way toward some anxious, uncertain, fragile hope. Unlike, say, the great Hans Urs von Balthasar (1905–1988), I would not think it worth the trouble to argue, as he does, that—given the paradoxes and seemingly irreconcilable pronouncements of scriptures on the final state of all things—Christians *may* be allowed to *dare* to hope for the salvation of all. In fact, I have very small patience for this kind of "hopeful universalism," as it is often called. As far as I am concerned, anyone who hopes for the universal reconciliation of creatures with God must already believe that this would be the best possible ending to the Christian story; and such a person has then no excuse for imagining that God could bring any but the best possible ending to pass without thereby being in some sense a failed creator. The position I want to attempt to argue, therefore, to see how well it holds together, is far more extreme: to wit, that, if Christianity is in any way true, Christians dare not *doubt* the salvation of all, and that any understanding of what God accomplished in Christ that does not include the assurance of a final *apokatastasis* in which all things created are redeemed and joined to God is ultimately entirely incoherent and unworthy of rational faith.

This is an exorbitant and somewhat insolent claim, I realize, and I would not make it if I did not earnestly believe every alternative view of the matter to be ultimately unsustainable. I think it, first of all, to be a claim that follows more or less ineluctably from any truly coherent contemplation of what it means to see God as the free creator of all things *ex nihilo*—especially when this doctrine is explicitly brought into connection with the question of the origins and ends of evil. The topic of evil, natural and moral, is obviously a difficult one, no matter how one approaches it; but it is a topic also that, treated candidly, confronts us with a very obvious equation, of crystalline clarity, whose final result I believe must prove to be either all or nothing (neither of which is a particularly tractable sum). I have written on the matter before, but generally have done so only from the side of creation, so to speak, in terms of how one should think about God from the vantage of the world we know. Thus I have always been able, as a rule, to beat a judicious retreat from the mystery of evil at just the right moment, and to seek a somewhat craven refuge in the classical metaphysics of divine transcendence—to which I remain entirely loyal, of course, but which can occasionally provide too easy an escape from some very terrible quandaries. The temptation to which I have often yielded has been simply to invoke the ontology of supereminence or divine impassibility or the eternal plenitude of the absolute (or what have you)—all of which reminds us that God *in se* is not determined by creation and that consequently evil does not enter into our understanding of the divine essence—and then to leave the matter there. Now, I still believe all those arguments to be true, as far as they go; but left to themselves they inexorably devolve toward half-truths, and then toward triviality: a wave of the prestidigitator's hand and Auschwitz magically vanishes. So I want to avoid the easy course on this occasion, and to address instead the other side of the metaphysical picture, the one that comes into view when we think not from the world to God, but from God to the world (to the very limited degree that we can do so): that is, the unavoidable conclusion that, precisely because God and creation are ontologically distinct from one another as the absolute and the contingent, they are morally indiscerptible.

Perhaps the first theological insight I learned from Gregory of Nyssa is that the Christian doctrine of *creatio ex nihilo* is not merely a cosmological or metaphysical claim, but also an eschatological claim about the world's relation to God, and for that reason a moral claim about the nature of God in himself. In the end of all things is their beginning, and only from the perspective of the end can one know what they are, why they have been made, and who the God is who has called them forth from nothingness. Anything willingly done is done toward an end; and anything done toward an end is defined by that end. And in Gregory's thought, with an integrity found only also in Origen and Maximus, protology and eschatology are a single science, a single revelation disclosed in the God-man. There is no profounder meditation on the meaning of creation than Gregory's eschatological treatise *On the Soul and Resurrection,* and no more brilliantly realized vision of the last things than his protological treatise *On the Making of Humanity.* For him, as is most clearly stated in the latter work, the cosmos will have been truly created only when it reaches its consummation in "the union of all things with the first Good," and humanity will have truly been created only when all human beings, united in the living body of Christ, become at last that "Godlike thing" that is "humankind according to the image." I shall talk about this at somewhat greater length in my Third Meditation, however.

Here my particular concern is the general principle that
the doctrine of creation constitutes an assertion regarding the
eternal identity of God. The doctrine in itself is, after all, chiefly
an affirmation of God's absolute dispositive liberty in all his
acts—the absence, that is, of any external restraint upon or
necessity behind every action of his will. And, while one must
avoid the pathetic anthropomorphism of imagining God's resolve to create as an arbitrary choice made after deliberation
among options, one must still affirm that it is free, that creation can add nothing to God, that God's being is not dependent on the world's, and that the only "necessity" present in
the divine act of creation is the impossibility of any hindrance
being placed upon God's expression of his own goodness in
making the world. Yet, for just this reason, the moral destiny
of creation and the moral nature of God are absolutely insepa-
rable. As the *transcendent* Good beyond all beings, God is also
the *transcendental* end that makes every single action of any
rational nature possible. Moreover, the end toward which he
acts must be his own goodness; for he is himself the beginning and end of all things. This is not to deny that, in addition
to the "primary causality" of God's act of creation, there are
innumerable forms of "secondary causality" operative within
the created order; but none of these can exceed or escape the
one end toward which the first cause directs all things. And
this eternal teleology that ultimately governs every action in
creation, viewed from the vantage of history, takes the form of
a cosmic eschatology. Seen as an eternal act of God, creation's
term is the divine nature for which all things were made; seen
from within the orientation of time, its term is the "final judgment" that brings all things to their true conclusion.

Moreover, no matter how great the autonomy one grants
the realm of secondary causes, two things are certain. First, as

God's act of creation is free, constrained by neither necessity nor ignorance, all contingent ends are intentionally enfolded within his decision. And, second, precisely because God in himself is absolute—"absolved," that is, of every pathos of the contingent, every "affect" of the sort that a finite substance has the power to visit upon another—his moral "venture" in creating is infinite. One way or another, after all, all causes are logically reducible to their first cause. This is no more than a logical truism. And it does not matter whether one construes the relation between primary and secondary causality as one of total determinism or as one of utter indeterminacy, for in either case all "consequents" are—either as actualities or merely as possibilities—contingent upon their primordial "antecedent," apart from which they could not exist. And, naturally, the rationale of a first cause—its "definition," in the most etymologically exact meaning of that term—is the *final* cause that prompts it, the end toward which it acts. If, then, that first cause is an infinitely free act emerging from an infinite wisdom, all those consequents are intentionally entailed— again, either as actualities or as possibilities—within that first act; and so the final end to which that act tends is its whole moral truth. The traditional ontological definition of evil as a *privatio boni*—a privation of the good lacking any essence of its own—is not merely a logically necessary metaphysical axiom about the transcendental structure of being; it is also an assertion that, when we say "God is good," we are speaking of him not only relative to his creation, but (however apophatically) as he is in himself. All comes from God, and so evil cannot be a "thing" that comes from anywhere. Evil is, in every case, merely the defect whereby a substantial good is lost, belied, or resisted. For in every sense being *is* act, and God, in his simplicity and infinite freedom, is what he does. He could not be the creator of anything substantially evil without evil also being part of the definition of who he essentially is; for he alone is the wellspring of all that exists.

Between the ontology of *creatio ex nihilo* and that of emanation, we should remember, there really is no metaphysical difference worth noting, unless by the latter we mean some kind of gross physical or material efflux of the divine substance into lesser substances (but of course no one, except perhaps John Milton, ever believed in such a thing). In either case, whether we are speaking of creation or emanation, all that exists comes from one divine source, and subsists by the divine grace of impartation and the creaturely labor of participation: an economy of donation and dependency, supereminence and individuation, actuality and potentiality. God goes forth in all beings and in all beings returns to himself, as even Aquinas (following a long Christian tradition) affirms; but God also does this not as an expression of his dialectical struggle with some recalcitrant exteriority—some external obstacle to be surmounted or some unrealized possibility to be achieved—but rather as the manifestation of an inexhaustible power wholly possessed by the divine in peaceful liberty in eternity. God has no need of the world; he creates it not because he is dependent upon it, but because its dependency on him is a fitting expression of the bounty of his goodness. So all that the doctrine of creation adds to the basic metaphysical picture is the further assurance that in this divine outpouring there is no element of the "irrational": nothing purely spontaneous, or organic, or even mechanical, beyond the power of God's rational freedom. This, however, also means that within the story of creation, viewed from its final cause, there can be no residue of the pardonably tragic, no irrecuperable or irreconcilable remainder left behind at the end of the tale; for, if there were, this irreconcilable excess would also be something God has directly caused, as an entailment freely assumed in his act of creating, and so as an expression of who he freely is. This is no more than the simple logic of the absolute. Hegel, for instance, saw the great slaughter-bench of history as a tragic inevitability in the Idea's odyssey toward *Geist* through the far countries of finite negation; for him, the merely particular — say, the isolated man whose death is, from the vantage of the all, no more consequential than the harvesting of a head of cabbage — is simply the smoke that rises from the sacrifice. The loss of the individual to the needs of the absolute remains in Hegel's system the "necessary surd," the meaningless remainder of a dialectical negation, which can be redeemed never in itself, but only *as* the negated, in the eternal identity of the divine.

Hegel's is a tale, though, no matter how one interprets it, of divine becoming, the great epic of "God" forging himself in the crucible of time. By contrast, the story Christians tell is of creation as God's sovereign act of love, neither adding to nor qualifying his eternal nature, and so it is also a story that leaves no room for an ultimate distinction between the universal truth of reason and the moral meaning of the particular, or for any distinction between the moral meaning of the particular and the moral nature of God. Precisely because God does not determine himself in creation — precisely because there is no dialectical necessity binding him to time or chaos, no need to shape his identity in the refining fires of history — in creating he reveals himself truly. Thus every evil that time comprises, natural or moral (which is, in this context, a largely worthless distinction, since human nature is a natural phenomenon), is an arraignment of God's goodness: every death of a child, every chance calamity, every act of malice;

everything diseased, thwarted, pitiless, purposeless, or cruel; and, until the end of all things, no answer has been given. Precisely because creation is not a theogony, all of it is theophany. It would be impious, I suppose, to suggest that, in his final divine judgment on his creatures, God will judge himself; but one must hold that by that judgment God will truly *disclose* himself (which, of course, is to say the same thing, in a more hushed and reverential voice). Even Paul dared to ask, in the tortured, conditional voice of the ninth chapter of Romans, whether there might be vessels of wrath stored up solely for destruction only because he trusted that there are not: because he believed instead that all are bound in disobedience, but only so that God might finally show mercy to all (Romans 11:32). If not for this radiant negative to the question Paul poses himself—this absolute rejection of the very idea that some souls exist only as exemplary objects of divine anger—he would not have been able at the last to affirm the perfect goodness of God in his saving works. Only by insisting upon the universality of God's mercy could Paul liberate himself from the fear that the particularity of that mercy would prove to be an ultimate injustice, and that in judging his creatures God would reveal himself not as the good God of faithfulness and love, but as an inconstant god who can shatter his own covenants at will. (To this I shall return in my Third Meditation.)

II

I have to note, however, that all of this creates a small problem of theological coherence, and for a rather obvious reason. To wit—and this should be an uncontroversial statement—the God in whom the majority of Christians throughout history have professed belief appears to be evil (at least, judging by the dreadful things they habitually say about him). And here I intend nothing more than an exercise in sober precision, based on the presumption that words should have some determinate content. Every putatively meaningful theological affirmation dangles upon a golden but fragile thread of analogy. On the one hand, this means that, for theology to have anything more than purely mythological content, it must be possible to speak of God without mistaking him for a being among beings, an instance of something greater than himself. Between God and creatures lies an epistemological chasm nothing less than infinite, which no predicate can span univocally. Even the followers of Duns Scotus (1266–1308), who have always believed that theological meaning must be secured within the weak embrace of a largely negative *conceptum univocum entis* (univocal concept of being), still also believe that the modal disproportion between the infinite and the finite renders the analogy between God and creatures irreducibly disjunctive. On the other hand, however, neither can theological language consist in nothing but equivocal expostulations, piously but fruitlessly offered up into the abyss of the divine mystery; it must employ words whose meanings do not simply melt away into nothingness at the threshold of the divine. Final equivocity would evacuate theological language not only of logical, but of semantic content; nothing could be affirmed—nothing would mean anything at all. And yet, down the centuries, Christians have again and again subscribed to formulations of their faith that clearly reduce a host of cardinal Christian theological usages—most especially moral predicates like "good," "merciful," "just," "benevolent," "loving"—to utter equivocity, and that by association reduce the entire grammar of Christian belief to meaninglessness. Indeed, so absolute is this equivocity that the only hope of rescuing any analogy from the general ruin would be to adopt "evil" as the sole plausible moral "pro-portion" between God and creatures. Here, at least, is a predi-cate whose semantic integrity can remain intact right to the very end of the story most Christians tell of God.

Nor am I speaking of a few marginal, eccentric sects within Christian history; I mean the broad mainstream: par-ticularly, I suppose it pleases me to say, but not exclusively, in the West. Let us, briefly, dwell on the obvious. Consider (to begin with the mildest of moral difficulties) how many Chris-tians down the centuries have had to reconcile their con-sciences to the repellant notion that all humans are at con-ception already guilty of a transgression that condemns them, justly, to eternal separation from God and eternal suffering, and that, in this doctrine's extreme form, every newborn in-fant belongs to a *massa damnata*, hateful in God's eyes from the first moment of existence. Really, no one should need to be told that this is a wicked claim: Gaze for a while at a newborn baby, and then try to believe earnestly and lovingly in such a God. If you find you are able to do so, then your religion has corrupted your conscience. But we can avoid affective argu-ments here. The claim is manifestly a contradiction in terms: The very notion of an "inherited guilt" is a logical absurdity, rather on the order of a "square circle." All that the doctrine can truly be taken to assert, speaking logically, is that God will-fully imputes to innocent creatures a guilt they can never have really contracted, out of what from any sane perspective can only be called malice. But this is just the beginning of the prob-lem. For one broad, venerable stream of tradition, God on the basis of this imputation consigns the vast majority of the race to perpetual torment, including infants who die unbaptized—though one later, intenerating redaction of the tale says that at least the youngest of these children, though forever denied

the supernatural bliss of the vision of God, will nonetheless
be granted the homely natural beatitude of the infants' limbo,
the *limbus infantium* (which mitigates but does not dispel the
doctrine's moral idiocy). And then the theology of "grace"
grows grimmer. For, according to the great Augustinian tradition, since we are somehow born meriting not only death
but eternal torment, we are enjoined to see and praise a laud-
able generosity in God's narrow choice to elect a small remnant
for salvation, before and apart from any consideration of their
concrete merits or demerits (*ante praevisa merita,* to use the
traditional formula), and his further choice either to predes-
tine or infallibly to surrender the vast remainder to everlasting
misery. When Augustine lamented the tenderheartedness, the
misericordia, that made Origen believe that demons, heathens,
and (most preposterously of all) unbaptized babies might ultimately be spared the torments of eternal fire, he made clear
how the moral imagination must bend and lacerate and twist
itself in order to absorb such beliefs. Pascal, in assuring us that
our existence is explicable only in light of a belief in the eternal and condign torment of babies who die before reaching
the baptismal font, shows us that there is often no meaningful
distinction between perfect faith and perfect nihilism. Calvin,
in telling us that hell is copiously populated with infants not a
cubit long, merely reminds us that, within a certain traditional
understanding of grace and predestination, the choice to worship God rather than the devil is at most a matter of prudence.
So it is that, for many Christians down the years, the rationale
of evangelization has been a desperate race to save as many
souls as possible *from God* (think of poor Francis Xavier, dying
of exhaustion trying to pluck as many infants as possible from
the flames of God's wrath).

Really, Reformed tradition is perhaps to be praised here,

if only for the flinty resolve with which it faces its creed's impli-
cations: Calvin, as I have noted, had the courage to acknowledge that his account of divine sovereignty necessitates belief
in the predestination not only of the saved and the damned,
but of the original fall of humankind itself; and he recognized
that the biblical claim that "God is love" must, on his principles, be accounted a definition not of God in himself, but
only of God as experienced by the elect (toward the damned,
God is in fact hate). And it is fitting that, among all models
of atonement, Reformed theology so securely fastened upon
a particularly sanguinary version of "substitution," one that
finds in the cross of Christ not simply God's self-outpouring
love, but also—and chiefly—the outpouring of his impla-
cable wrath against sin. And then even this act of substitution turns out to be one of a peculiarly miserly kind, since
its appeasements avail for only a very few. An eternal hell is
still required for the great many, in order to reveal the glory
of divine sovereignty in its fullness. Very well. So this side of
Calvinism is nothing but a savage *reductio ad absurdum* of the
worst aspects of an immensely influential but still deeply defective theological tradition. (And I could here, if I wanted to
do so, play the loftily supercilious Eastern Orthodox and denounce these doctrinal deformations as just so much Western
Christian "barbarism," and then slowly, haughtily turn away
and make my indignant retreat to the pre-Augustinian idyll
of Byzantine theology.) And, needless to say, the brute invoca-
tion of divine sovereignty as an argument for the moral intelligibility of hell exercised a more immediate logical appeal in
the days when the heathen cult of class still held sway over the
better part of humanity's moral imagination, and when men
and women were accustomed to servile cringing before the
arbitrary whims of potentates, and to offering up obsequious

encomia to their masters' "divine right" and "absolute sovereignty" and squalid nonsense of that kind. Surely, though — so we might want to tell ourselves — these are aberrations. Surely, having duly acknowledged the unfortunate contingencies of cultural history, we need not grant that the larger Christian understanding of God is morally contradictory. Bad theology does not invalidate true faith; *abusus non tollit usum,* after all.

Would that the matter were quite that simple. The truth is that all of these theological degeneracies follow from an incoherence deeply fixed at the heart of almost all Christian traditions: that is, the idea that the omnipotent God of love, who creates the world from nothing, either imposes or tolerates the eternal torment of the damned. It was not merely peculiarity of personal temperament that prompted Tertullian (c. 155–c. 240) to speak of the saved relishing the delightful spectacle of the destruction of the reprobate, or that prompted Peter Lombard (c. 1096–1160) and Thomas Aquinas (1225–1274) to assert that the vision of the torments of the damned will increase the beatitude of the redeemed (as any trace of pity would darken the joys of heaven), or that prompted Martin Luther (1483–1546) to insist that the saved will rejoice to see their loved ones roasting in hell. None of these good pious souls was doing anything other than following the only poor thread of logic he had to guide him out of a labyrinth of impossible contradictions; the sheer enormity of the idea of a hell of eternal torment forces the mind toward absurdities and atrocities. But, long before the moral issues even come into view, the logical deficiencies in such language should already be obvious: After all, what is a person other than a whole history of associations, loves, memories, attachments, and affinities? Who are we, other than all the others who have made us who we are, and to whom we belong as much as they to us? We *are* those others. To say

that the sufferings of the damned will either be clouded from
the eyes of the blessed or, worse, increase the pitiless bliss of
heaven is also to say that *no* persons can possibly be saved: for,
if the memories of others are removed, or lost, or one's knowledge of their misery is converted into indifference or, God forbid, into greater beatitude, what then remains of one in one's
last bliss? Some other being altogether, surely: a spiritual ano-
nymity, a vapid spark of pure intellection, the residue of a soul
that has been reduced to no one. Not, however, a person—not
the person who was. But I shall return to that issue in my Third
Meditation. Here it suffices to note that, in the end, the deepest
problem with such claims is not so much their logic as their
sheer moral hideousness.

III

The most civilized apologists for the "infernalist" orthodoxies
these days, as I have noted elsewhere in these pages, tend to
prefer to defend their position by an appeal to creaturely freedom and to God's respect for its dignity. And, as I have also
noted, there could scarcely be a poorer argument; whether
made crudely or elegantly, it invariably fails, because it depends upon an incoherent model of freedom. If one could
plausibly explain how an absolutely libertarian act, obedient to
no prior rationale whatsoever, would be distinguishable from
sheer chance, or a mindless organic or mechanical impulse,
and so any more "free" than an earthquake or embolism, then
the argument might carry some weight. But to me it seems impossible to speak of freedom in any meaningful sense at all unless one begins from the assumption that, for a rational spirit,
to see the good and know it truly is to desire it insatiably and
to obey it unconditionally, while not to desire it is not to have

known it truly, and so never to have been free to choose it. I can defer the full philosophical argument to my Fourth Meditation. But here I can at least point out that scripture seems to support my view. "And you will know the truth, and the truth will make you free" (John 8:32): for freedom and truth are one, and not to know the truth is to be enslaved. "Father, forgive them; for they do not know what they are doing" (Luke 23:34): not seeing the Good, says God to God, they did not freely choose evil, and must be pardoned. "Everyone committing sin is a slave to sin" (John 8:34): and a slave, needless to say, is not free. Moreover, it is simply obvious that, under normal conditions, we recognize any self-destructive impulse in any person as a form of madness. It makes no more sense, then, to say that God allows creatures to damn themselves out of his love for them or out of his respect for their freedom than to say a father might reasonably allow his deranged child to thrust her face into a fire out of a tender regard for her moral autonomy. And, as absurd as is the idea of someone "in a right mind" choosing eternal loneliness and torment rather than eternal love and bliss, the argument becomes all the more insufferably ludicrous when one considers the personal conditions—ignorance, mortality, defectibility of intellect and will—under which each soul enters the world, and the circumstances—the suffering of all creatures, even the most innocent and delightful of them—with which that world confronts the soul. But all of this can wait for now. In a sense, none of it matters at this point, as the issue of creaturely freedom makes no difference as regards my argument here.

Again, let me say, I think Reformed tradition is commendable in this regard for the simple intellectual honesty with which it elevates divine sovereignty to the status of *the* absolute theological value, and sovereignty understood as pure inscrutable power. But, alas, honesty is not the same thing as cogency. The epistemological cost of this candor is enormous—to the point, in fact, of a total impoverishment— because Reformed theology is still dogmatically obliged to ascribe to God all those predicates (except "love," apparently) that scripture supplies, and so must call God "good," "just," "merciful," "wise," and "truthful." But, transparently, all these terms have been rendered equivocal by the doctrines that surround them, and this equivocity is necessarily contagious; it reduces *all* theological language to vacuity, for none of it can now be trusted. The system, in the end, is one devoid of logical or semantic content: it means nothing, it can be neither believed nor doubted, it is just a formal arrangement of intrinsically empty signifiers, no more true or false than any other purely abstract pattern. And obviously no refuge is offered by the stern teaching of the human intellect's "total depravity," as that merely reiterates the problem of equivocity, albeit with a decorous dressing of ceremonious cringing. If faith is really so devoid of evident rationality, then it is not even faith, for it possesses no intelligible content. Thus, even if the traditional Calvinist were right, he would be wrong for believing he was right. In the words of John Stuart Mill (in his *An Examination of Sir William Hamilton's Philosophy*), "To say that God's goodness may be different in kind from man's goodness, what is it but saying, with a slight change of phraseology, that God may possibly not be good?" Again, however, it is not only Reformed theology that suffers from this contagion of equivocity; it infects every theology that includes the notion of an eternal hell—which is to say, just about the whole Christian tradition.

This is not a complicated issue, it seems to me: The eternal perdition—the eternal suffering—of any soul would be an abominable tragedy, and therefore a profound natural evil; this much is stated quite clearly by scripture, in asserting that God "intends all human beings to be saved and to come to a full knowledge of truth" (1 Timothy 2:4). A natural evil, however, becomes a moral evil precisely to the degree that it is the positive intention, even if only conditionally, of a rational will. God could not, then, directly intend a soul's ultimate destruction, or even intend that a soul bring about its own destruction, without positively willing the evil end *as* an evil end; such a result could not possibly be comprised within the ends purposed by a truly good will (in any sense of the word "good" intelligible to us). Yet, if both the doctrine of *creatio ex nihilo* and that of eternal damnation are true, that very evil is indeed already comprised within the *positive* intentions and dispositions of God. No refuge is offered here by some specious distinction between God's antecedent and consequent wills—between, that is, his universal will for creation apart from the fall and his particular will regarding each creature in consequence of the fall. Under the canopy of God's omnipotence and omniscience, the consequent is already wholly virtually present in the antecedent. Nor, for the same reason, does it help here to draw a distinction between evils that are positively willed and evils that are providentially permitted for the sake of some greater good. A greater good is by definition a conditional and therefore relative good; its conditions are already and inalienably part of its positive content. Moreover, in this case, the evil by which this putative good has been accomplished must be accounted an eternally present condition within that good, since an endless punishment is—at least for the soul that experiences it—an end intended in itself. This evil, then, must remain forever the "other side" of whatever good it might help to bring about. So, while we may no doubt hope that some limited good will emerge from the cosmic drama, one that is somehow preponderant over the evil, limited it must forever remain; at such an unspeakable and irrecuperable cost, it can be at best only a tragically ambiguous good. This is the price of creation, it would seem. God, on this view, has "made a bargain" with a natural evil. He has willed the tragedy, not just as a transient dissonance within creation's goodness, leading ultimately to a soul's correction, but as that irreducible quantum of eternal loss that, however small in relation to the whole, still reduces all else to a merely relative value.

What then, we might well ask, does this make of the story of salvation—of its cost? What would any damned soul be, after all, as enfolded within the eternal will of God, other than a price settled upon by God with his own power, an oblation willingly exchanged for a finite benefit—the lamb slain from the foundation of the world? And is hell not then the innermost secret of heaven, its sacrificial heart? And what then is God's moral nature, inasmuch as the moral character of any intended final cause must include within its calculus what one is willing to sacrifice to achieve that end; and, if the "acceptable" price is the eternal torment of a rational nature, what room remains for any moral analogy comprehensible within finite terms? After all, the economics of the exchange is as monstrous as it is exact. We can all appreciate, I imagine, the shattering force of Vanya's terrible question to Alyosha in *The Brothers Karamazov*: If universal harmony and joy could be secured by the torture and murder of a single innocent child, would you accept that price? But let us stipulate that, perhaps, in the context of Dostoevsky's novel, somehow, mysteriously—in, say, Zosima's sanctity, Alyosha's kiss of Vanya, the quadrillion-kilometer march of Vanya's devil, the callous old woman's onion—an answer is offered that might make the transient torments of history justifiable in the light of God's everlasting Kingdom. I do not think this is true, but for the sake of the argument let us suppose it is so. But *eternal* torments, *final* dereliction? Here the price is raised beyond any calculus of relative goods, and into the realm of absolute—of infinite—expenditure.

The arithmetic, moreover, is fairly inflexible. We need not imagine, in traditional fashion, that the legions of the damned will far outnumber the cozy company of the saved. Let us imagine instead that only one soul will perish eternally, and all others enter into the peace of the Kingdom. Nor need we think of that soul as guiltless, like Vanya's helpless child, or even as mildly sympathetic. Let it be someone utterly despicable—say, Hitler. Even then, no matter how we understand the fate of that single wretched soul in relation to God's intentions, no account of the divine decision to create out of nothingness can make its propriety morally intelligible. This is obvious, of course, in predestinarian systems, since from their bleak perspective, manifestly, that poor, ridiculous, but tragically conscious puppet who has been consigned to the abyss exists for no other purpose than the ghastly spectacle of divine sovereignty. But, then, for the redeemed, each of whom might just as well have been denied efficacious grace had God so pleased (since no one merits salvation), who is that wretch who endures God's final wrath, forever and ever, other than their surrogate, their redeemer, the one who suffers in their stead— their Christ? For what it is worth, I for one do not object in the least to Hitler being purged of his sins and saved, over however many aeons of inconceivably painful purification in hell that might take, but I do most definitely object to Hitler fixed forever in his sins serving as my redeemer in some shadow eternity of perpetual torment, offering up his screams of agony as the price of my hope for salvation. The very thought reduces all the central articles of the Christian faith to cheap trifles. Compared to that unspeakable offering, after all, that interminable and abominable oblation of infinite misery, what would the cross of Christ be? How would it be diminished for us? And to what? A bad afternoon? A vanishingly temporary indisposition of the infinite? And what would the mystery of God becoming a man in order to effect a merely partial rescue of created order truly be, as compared to the far deeper mystery of a worthless man becoming the suffering god upon whose perpetual holocaust the entire order of creation finally depends? A smaller gesture within the greater? A minor, local economy within the totality of the universal?

Predestination, in fact, need not be invoked here at all. Brush the issue entirely aside. Let us suppose instead that rational creatures possess real autonomy of almost godlike scope, and that no one goes to hell save by his or her own Promethean industry and ingenuity: When we then look at God's decision to create from that angle, we find, curiously enough, that absolutely nothing changes. Not to wax too anthropomorphizing here, like a poor simpleminded analytic philosopher of religion who thinks of God as some immense finite agent similar to us (if much more imposing), but we really should pause to interrogate the logic of God's motives in the story as commonly told. Let us, that is, say God created simply *on the chance* that humanity might sin, and *on the chance* that a certain number of incorrigibly wicked souls might plunge themselves into the fiery abyss forever. This still means that, morally, he has purchased the revelation of his power in creation by the same horrendous price—even if, in the end, no one at all should happen to be damned. The logic is irresistible. God creates. The die is cast. *Alea iacta est.* But then again, as Mallarmé says, "Un coup de dés jamais n'abolira le hasard"

(A throw of the dice will never abolish the hazard): for what is hazarded has already been surrendered, entirely, no matter how the dice may fall. The outcome of the aleatory venture may be intentionally indeterminate, but the wager itself is an irrevocable intentional decision, wherein every possible cost has already been accepted; the irrecuperable expenditure has been offered even if, happily, it is never actually lost, and so the moral nature of the act is the same in either case. To venture the life of your child for some other end is, morally, already to have killed your child, even if at the last moment Artemis or Heracles or the Angel of the LORD should stay your hand. And so, the revelation of God's glory in creatures would still always be dependent upon that evil, or that venture *beyond* good and evil, even if at the last no one should perish. Creation could never then be called "good" in an unconditional sense; nor God the "Good as such," no matter what conditional goods he might accomplish in creating. And, here too, the losing lot might just as well have fallen to the blessed, given the stochastic vagaries of existence: accidents of birth, congenital qualities of character, natural intellectual endowments, native moral aptitudes, material circumstances, personal powers of resolve, impersonal forces of chance, the grim encumbrances of sin and mortality . . . The saved might, by this or that small twist of fate or folly, have been the damned, and the damned the saved. Once again, then, who would the damned be but the redeemers of the blessed, the price eternally paid by God for the sake of the Kingdom's felicity?

Nor does the arithmetic change very much—at least, not nearly as much as one might hope—if one gives up on the idea of a hell of eternal torment and poses in its place a final "hell" consisting in the ultimate annihilation of evildoers at the end of days. Admittedly, the latter idea is considerably more palatable than the former; and, for what it is worth, it also appears to accord somewhat better with the large majority of scriptural metaphors, the dominical metaphors in particular, for final damnation. But such an eventuality would still be an irreducible price exacted, a sacrifice eternally preserved in the economy of God's Kingdom. The ultimate absence of a certain number of created rational natures would still be a kind of last end inscribed in God's eternity, a measure of failure or loss forever preserved within the totality of the tale of divine victory. If what is lost is lost finally and absolutely, then whatever remains, however glorious, is the residue of an unresolved and no less ultimate tragedy, and so could constitute only a contingent and relative "happy ending." Seen in that way, the lost are still the price that God has contracted from everlasting—whether by predestination or mere permission—for the sake of his Kingdom; and so it remains a Kingdom founded upon both an original and a final sacrificial exclusion. In either case—eternal torment, eternal oblivion—creation and redemption are negotiations with evil, death, and suffering, and so never in an absolute sense God's good working of all things. I shall touch on this again.

To be clear, though, I am not attempting to subject God to an "ethical" interrogation, as though he were some finite agent answerable to standards beyond himself. That would be banal. This sort of exercise in "game theory," so to speak—this unfolding of the implicit "rules" of God's creative acts—relies upon perilous metaphors and risks silly anthropomorphisms, granted. But the imagery of the argument is illustrative only of a single logical point about absolute or relative values, in either victory or defeat; it should not be taken as a literal depiction of how God "behaves," as though he really were some sort of finite psychological subject deliberating among differ-

ent courses of action, trying to decide precisely what he is willing to lose at the tables. My concern is the coherence of theological language in light of the logically indispensable doctrine
of *creatio ex nihilo*. The golden thread of analogy can stretch
across as vast an apophatic abyss as the modal disjunction between infinite and finite or the ontological disproportion between absolute and contingent can open before us; but it cannot span a total antithesis. When we use words like "good,"
"just," "love" to name God, not as if they are mysteriously
greater in meaning than when predicated of creatures, but instead as if they bear transparently *opposite* meanings, then we
are saying nothing. And, again, the contagion of this equivocity necessarily consumes theology entirely.

IV

Of course, theological language is determined by scripture. I
shall touch upon a number (though not all) of the New Testament's most famously universalist verses in a moment, in my
Second Meditation, and especially upon those that clearly assert a strict equivalence between what is lost in Adam and what
is saved in Christ. I shall simply observe at this point how odd
it is that for at least fifteen centuries such passages have been
all but lost behind a veil as thin as the one that can be woven
from those three or four deeply ambiguous verses that seem
(and only *seem*) to threaten eternal torments for the wicked.
But that is as may be. Every good New Testament scholar is
well aware of the obscurities that throng every attempt to re-
construct the eschatological vision described in Jesus's teachings or in the other books of the New Testament canon. And,
anyway, plucking individual verses like posies here and there
from the text is no way to gain a proper view of the entire

landscape. The New Testament, to a great degree, consists in an eschatological interpretation of Hebrew scripture's story of creation, finding in Christ, as eternal Logos and risen Lord, the unifying term of beginning and end. For Paul in particular, the marvel of Christ's lordship is that all walls of division between persons and peoples, and finally between all creatures, have fallen, and that ultimately, when creation is restored by Christ, God will be all in all. There is no more magnificent meditation on this vision than Gregory of Nyssa's description of the progress of all persons toward union with God in the one *plē-rōma*, the one fullness, of the "whole Christ": all spiritual wills moving, to use his lovely image, from outside the temple walls (in the ages) into the temple precincts, and finally (beyond the ages) into the very sanctuary of the glory—as one. By contrast, Augustine, in the last masterpiece produced by his colossal genius, wrote of two cities eternally sealed against one another, from everlasting in the divine counsels and unto everlasting in the divine judgment (the far more populous city destined for perpetual sorrow). There is no question in my mind which of them saw the story more clearly, or who came nearer the heart of the gospel. Nor do I doubt which theologians are the best guides to scripture as a whole: Gregory, Origen, Evagrius, Theodore of Mopsuestia, Diodore of Tarsus, Isaac of Nineveh . . . George MacDonald.

Here, however, again, the issue is the reducibility of all causes to their first cause, and the determination of the first cause by the final, which is also by extension the issue of God's primordial "venture" in calling all things into being freely. If Christians did not proclaim a *creatio ex nihilo*—if they thought God a being limited by some external principle or internal imperfection, or if they were dualists, or dialectical idealists, or what have you—the question of evil would be an aetiological

query only for them, not a terrible moral conundrum. But, because they say God creates freely, they must believe that his
final judgment shall reveal him for who he is. And as God is
act—as are we all in some sense—and as God is what he does,
if there is a final irreconcilable dual result to his act in creating, then there is also an original irreconcilable dual premise stretching all the way back into the divine nature. So, if all
are not saved, if God creates souls he knows to be destined for
eternal misery, is God evil? Well, perhaps one might conclude
instead that he is both good and evil, or that he is beyond good
and evil altogether, which is to say beyond the supremacy of the
Good; but, then again, to stand outside the sovereignty of the
Good is in fact to be evil after all, so it all amounts to the same
thing. But maybe every analogy ultimately fails. What is not
debatable is that, if God does so create, in himself he cannot
be the Good as such, and creation cannot be a morally meaningful act: It is, seen from one vantage, an act of predilective
love; but, seen from another—logically necessary—vantage, it
is an act of prudential malevolence. And so it cannot be true.
We are presented by what has become the majority tradition
with three fundamental claims, any two of which might be true
simultaneously, but never all three: that God freely created all
things out of nothingness; that God is the Good itself; and that
it is certain or at least possible that some rational creatures will
endure eternal loss of God. And this, I have to say, is the final
moral meaning I find in the doctrine of *creatio ex nihilo,* at
least if one truly believes that traditional Christian language
about God's goodness and the theological grammar to which it
belongs are not empty: that the God of eternal retribution and
pure sovereignty proclaimed by so much of Christian tradition
is not, and cannot possibly be, the God of self-outpouring love
revealed in Christ. If God is the good creator of all, he must

also be the savior of all, without fail, who brings to himself all he has made, including all rational wills, and only thus returns to himself in all that goes forth from him. If he is not the savior of all, the Kingdom is only a dream, and creation something considerably worse than a nightmare. But, again, it is not so. According to scripture, God saw that what he created was good. If so, then all creatures must, in the ages, see it as well.

Second Meditation

What Is Judgment?

A Reflection on Biblical Eschatology

I

Needless to say, the question of Christian universalism, or at least of its theological liceity, cannot be addressed without a long, perhaps even interminable contemplation of the eschatological language and imagery and promises of scripture. I am not very tolerant of what is sometimes called "biblicism" — that is, the "oracular" understanding of scriptural inspiration, which sees the Bible as the record of words directly uttered by the lips of God through an otherwise dispensable human intermediary, and which entails the belief that the testimony of the Bible on doctrinal and theological matters must be wholly internally consistent — and I certainly have no patience whatsoever for twentieth-century biblical fundamentalism and its manifest imbecilities. Neither, however, am I so recklessly speculative as to imagine that Christians are allowed to make any theological pronouncements in total abstraction from or contradiction of scripture. And, while I dislike the practice of reducing biblical theology to concentrated distillates — "proof texts," that is—I gladly concede that, at the very least, a certain presumptive authority has to be granted to whatever kind of language the Bible uses most preponderantly. This, though, is not nearly as simple a matter as one might imagine.

There is a general sense among most Christians that the notion of an eternal hell is explicitly and unremittingly advanced in the New Testament; and yet, when we go looking for it in the actual pages of the text, it proves remarkably elusive. The whole idea is, for instance, entirely absent from the Pauline corpus, as even the thinnest shadow of a hint. Nor is it anywhere patently present in any of the other epistolary texts. There is one verse in the gospels, Matthew 25:46, that—at least, as traditionally understood—offers what seems the strongest evidence for the idea (though even there, as I shall explain below, the wording leaves room for considerable doubt regarding its true significance); and then there are perhaps a couple of verses from Revelation (though, as ever when dealing with that particular book, *caveat lector*). Beyond that, nothing is clear. What in fact the New Testament provides us with are a number of fragmentary and fantastic images that can be taken in any number of ways, arranged according to our prejudices and expectations, and declared literal or figural or hyperbolic as our desires dictate. True, Jesus speaks of a final judgment, and uses many metaphors to describe the unhappy lot of the condemned. Many of these are metaphors of destruction, like the annihilation of chaff or brambles in ovens, or the final death of body and soul in the Valley of Hinnom (Gehenna). Others are metaphors of exclusion, like the sealed doors of wedding feasts. A few, a very few, are images of imprisonment and torture; but, even then, in the relevant verses, those punishments are depicted as having only a limited term

(Matthew 5:36; 18:34; Luke 12:47–48, 59). Nowhere is there any description of a kingdom of perpetual cruelty presided over by Satan, as though he were a kind of chthonian god.

On the other hand, however, there are a remarkable number of passages in the New Testament, several of them from Paul's writings, that appear instead to promise a final salvation of all persons and all things, and in the most unqualified terms. I imagine some or most of these latter could be explained away as rhetorical exaggeration; but then, presumably, the same could be said of those verses that appear to presage an everlasting division between the redeemed and the reprobate. To me it is surpassingly strange that, down the centuries, most Christians have come to believe that one class of claims—all of which are allegorical, pictorial, vague, and metaphorical in form—must be regarded as providing the "literal" content of the New Testament's teaching regarding the world to come, while another class—all of which are invariably straightforward doctrinal statements—must be regarded as mere hyperbole. It is one of the great mysteries of Christian history (or perhaps of a certain kind of religious psychopathology). And it is certainly curious also that so many Christians are able to recognize that the language of scripture is full of metaphor, on just about every page, and yet fail to notice that, when it comes to descriptions of the world to come, there are no nonmetaphorical images at all. Why precisely this should be I cannot say. We can see that the ovens are metaphors, and the wheat and the chaff, and the angelic harvest, and the barred doors, and the debtors' prisons; so why do we not also recognize that the deathless worm and the inextinguishable fire and all other such images (none of which, again, means quite what the infernalist imagines) are themselves mere figural devices within the embrace of an extravagant apocalyptic imagery that, in itself, has no strictly literal elements? How did some images become *mere* images in the general Christian imagination while others became exact documentary portraits of some final reality? If one can be swayed simply by the brute force of arithmetic, it seems worth noting that, among the apparently most explicit statements on the last things, the universalist statements are by far the more numerous. I am thinking of such verses as, say:

Romans 5:18–19: Ἄρα οὖν ὡς δι᾽ ἑνὸς παραπτώματος εἰς πάντας ἀνθρώπους εἰς κατάκριμα, οὕτως καὶ δι᾽ ἑνὸς δικαιώματος εἰς πάντας ἀνθρώπους εἰς δικαίωσιν ζωῆς· ὥσπερ γὰρ διὰ τῆς παρακοῆς τοῦ ἑνὸς ἀνθρώπου ἁμαρτωλοὶ κατεστάθησαν οἱ πολλοί, οὕτως καὶ διὰ τῆς ὑπακοῆς τοῦ ἑνὸς δίκαιοι κατασταθήσονται οἱ πολλοί. (So, then, just as through one transgression came condemnation for all human beings, so also through one act of righteousness came a rectification of life for all human beings; for, just as by the heedlessness of the one man the many were rendered sinners, so also by the obedience of the one the many will be rendered righteous.)

Or:

1 Corinthians 15:22: ὥσπερ γὰρ ἐν τῷ Ἀδὰμ πάντες ἀποθνῄσκουσιν, οὕτως καὶ ἐν τῷ Χριστῷ πάντες ζωοποιηθήσονται. (For just as in Adam all die, so also in the Anointed [Christ] all will be given life.)

Or:

2 Corinthians 5:14: ἡ γὰρ ἀγάπη τοῦ Χριστοῦ
συνέχει ἡμᾶς, κρίναντας τοῦτο, ὅτι εἷς ὑπὲρ
πάντων ἀπέθανεν, ἄρα οἱ πάντες ἀπέθανον . . .
(For the love of the Anointed constrains us, having
reached this judgment: that one died on behalf of
all; all then have died . . .)

Or even:

Romans 11:32: συνέκλεισεν γὰρ ὁ θεὸς τοὺς πάντας
εἰς ἀπείθειαν ἵνα τοὺς πάντας ἐλεήσῃ. (For God
shut up everyone in obstinacy so that he might
show mercy to everyone.)

Or, of course:

1 Timothy 2:3-6: . . . τοῦ σωτῆρος ἡμῶν θεοῦ, ὃς
πάντας ἀνθρώπους θέλει σωθῆναι καὶ εἰς ἐπίγνωσιν
ἀληθείας ἐλθεῖν. Εἷς γὰρ θεός, εἷς καὶ μεσίτης θεοῦ
καὶ ἀνθρώπων, ἄνθρωπος Χριστὸς Ἰησοῦς, ὁ δοὺς
ἑαυτὸν ἀντίλυτρον ὑπὲρ πάντων . . . (. . . our savior
God, who intends all human beings to be saved and
to come to a full knowledge of truth. For there is
one God, and also one mediator of God and human
beings: a human being, the Anointed One Jesus,
who gave himself as a liberation fee for all . . .)

And:

Titus 2:11: Ἐπεφάνη γὰρ ἡ χάρις τοῦ θεοῦ σωτήριος
πᾶσιν ἀνθρώποις . . . (For the grace of God has appeared, giving salvation to all human beings . . .)

And:

> 2 Corinthians 5:19: ὡς ὅτι θεὸς ἦν ἐν Χριστῷ κόσμον καταλλάσσων ἑαυτῷ, μὴ λογιζόμενος αὐτοῖς τὰ παραπτώματα αὐτῶν καὶ θέμενος ἐν ἡμῖν τὸν λόγον τῆς καταλλαγῆς. (Thus God was in the Anointed reconciling the cosmos to himself, not accounting their trespasses to them, and placing in us the word of reconciliation.)

As well as:

> Ephesians 1:9–10: γνωρίσας ἡμῖν τὸ μυστήριον τοῦ θελήματος αὐτοῦ, κατὰ τὴν εὐδοκίαν αὐτοῦ ἣν προέθετο ἐν αὐτῷ εἰς οἰκονομίαν τοῦ πληρώματος τῶν καιρῶν, ἀνακεφαλαιώσασθαι τὰ πάντα ἐν τῷ Χριστῷ, τὰ ἐπὶ τοῖς οὐρανοῖς καὶ τὰ ἐπὶ τῆς γῆς . . . (Making known to us the mystery of his will, which was his purpose in him, for a husbandry of the seasons' fullness, to recapitulate all things in the Anointed, the things in the heavens and the things on earth . . .)

And presumably:

> Colossians 1:27–28: οἷς ἠθέλησεν ὁ θεὸς γνωρίσαι τί τὸ πλοῦτος τῆς δόξης τοῦ μυστηρίου τούτου ἐν τοῖς ἔθνεσιν, ὅ ἐστιν Χριστὸς ἐν ὑμῖν, ἡ ἐλπὶς τῆς δόξης· ὃν ἡμεῖς καταγγέλλομεν νουθετοῦντες πάντα ἄνθρωπον καὶ διδάσκοντες πάντα ἄνθρωπον ἐν πάσῃ σοφίᾳ, ἵνα παραστήσωμεν πάντα ἄνθρωπον τέλειον ἐν Χριστῷ . . . (By whom

God wished to make known what the wealth of this mystery's glory is among the gentiles, which is the Anointed within you, the hope of glory, whom we proclaim, warning every human being and teaching every human being in all wisdom, so that we may present every human being as perfected in the Anointed . . .)

And surely:

John 12:32: κἀγὼ ἐὰν ὑψωθῶ ἐκ τῆς γῆς, πάντας ἑλκύσω πρὸς ἐμαυτόν. (And I, when I am lifted up from the earth, will drag everyone to me.)

And perhaps:

Hebrews 2:9: τὸν δὲ βραχύ τι παρ᾽ ἀγγέλους ἠλαττωμένον βλέπομεν Ἰησοῦν διὰ τὸ πάθημα τοῦ θανάτου δόξῃ καὶ τιμῇ ἐστεφανωμένον, ὅπως χάριτι θεοῦ ὑπὲρ παντὸς γεύσηται θανάτου. (But we see Jesus, who was made just a little less than angels, having been crowned with glory and honor on account of suffering death, so that by God's grace he might taste of death on behalf of everyone.)

And then there is this elegantly condensed syllogism (or enthymeme):

John 17:2: καθὼς ἔδωκας αὐτῷ ἐξουσίαν πάσης σαρκός, ἵνα πᾶν ὃ δέδωκας αὐτῷ δώσῃ αὐτοῖς ζωὴν αἰώνιον. (Just as you gave him power over all flesh, so that you have given everything to him, that he might give them life in the Age.)

And this:

John 4:42: τῇ τε γυναικὶ ἔλεγον ὅτι οὐκέτι διὰ τὴν σὴν λαλιὰν πιστεύομεν, αὐτοὶ γὰρ ἀκηκόαμεν καὶ οἴδαμεν ὅτι οὗτός ἐστιν ἀληθῶς ὁ σωτὴρ τοῦ κόσμου. (And they said to the woman: "We no longer have faith on account of your talk; for we ourselves have listened and we know that this man is truly the savior of the cosmos.")

Which is confirmed in:

John 12:47: ... οὐ γὰρ ἦλθον ἵνα κρίνω τὸν κόσμον, ἀλλ᾽ ἵνα σώσω τὸν κόσμον. (... for I came not that I might judge the cosmos, but that I might save the cosmos.)

And:

1 John 4:14: καὶ ἡμεῖς τεθεάμεθα καὶ μαρτυροῦμεν ὅτι ὁ πατὴρ ἀπέσταλκεν τὸν υἱὸν σωτῆρα τοῦ κόσμου. (And we have seen and attest that the Father has sent the Son as savior of the cosmos.)

There is, as well:

2 Peter 3:9: οὐ βραδύνει κύριος τῆς ἐπαγγελίας, ὥς τινες βραδύτητα ἡγοῦνται, ἀλλὰ μακροθυμεῖ

εἰς ὑμᾶς μὴ βουλόμενός τινας ἀπολέσθαι ἀλλὰ πάντας εἰς μετάνοιαν χωρῆσαι. (The Lord is not delaying what is promised, as some reckon delay, but is magnanimous toward you, intending for no one to perish, but rather for all to advance to a change of heart.)

Maybe even:

Matthew 18:14: οὕτως οὐκ ἔστιν θέλημα ἔμπροσθεν τοῦ πατρὸς ὑμῶν τοῦ ἐν οὐρανοῖς ἵνα ἀπόληται ἓν τῶν μικρῶν τούτων. (So it is not a desire that occurs to your Father in the heavens that one of these little ones should perish.)

And:

Philippians 2:9–11: διὸ καὶ ὁ θεὸς αὐτὸν ὑπερύψωσεν καὶ ἐχαρίσατο αὐτῷ τὸ ὄνομα τὸ ὑπὲρ πᾶν ὄνομα, ἵνα ἐν τῷ ὀνόματι Ἰησοῦ πᾶν γόνυ κάμψῃ ἐπουρανίων καὶ ἐπιγείων καὶ καταχθονίων καὶ πᾶσα γλῶσσα ἐξομολογήσηται ὅτι κύριος Ἰησοῦς Χριστὸς εἰς δόξαν θεοῦ πατρός. (For which reason God also exalted him on high and graced him with the name that is above every name, so that at the name of Jesus every knee should bend—of beings heavenly and earthly and subterranean—and every tongue gladly confess that Jesus the Anointed is Lord, for the glory of God the Father.)

And:

> Colossians 1:19–20: ὅτι ἐν αὐτῷ εὐδόκησεν πᾶν τὸ
> πλήρωμα κατοικῆσαι καὶ δι᾽ αὐτοῦ ποκαταλλάξαι
> τὰ πάντα εἰς αὐτόν, εἰρηνοποιήσας διὰ τοῦ
> αἵματος τοῦ σταυροῦ αὐτοῦ, [δι᾽ αὐτοῦ] εἴτε τὰ
> ἐπὶ τῆς γῆς εἴτε τὰ ἐν τοῖς οὐρανοῖς. (For in him
> all the Fullness was pleased to take up a dwelling,
> and through him to reconcile all things to him,
> making peace by the blood of his cross [through
> him], whether the things on the earth or the things
> in the heavens.)

And most definitely:

> 1 John 2:2: καὶ αὐτὸς ἱλασμός ἐστιν περὶ τῶν
> ἁμαρτιῶν ἡμῶν, οὐ περὶ τῶν ἡμετέρων δὲ μόνον
> ἀλλὰ καὶ περὶ ὅλου τοῦ κόσμου. (And he is atone-
> ment for our sins, and not only for ours, but for the
> whole cosmos.)

And such mysterious verses as:

> John 3:17: οὐ γὰρ ἀπέστειλεν ὁ θεὸς τὸν υἱὸν εἰς
> τὸν κόσμον ἵνα κρίνῃ τὸν κόσμον, ἀλλ᾽ ἵνα σωθῇ
> ὁ κόσμος δι᾽ αὐτοῦ. (For God sent the Son into the
> cosmos not that he might condemn the cosmos,
> but that the cosmos might be saved through him.)

And:

> Luke 16:16: Ὁ νόμος καὶ οἱ προφῆται μέχρι Ἰωάννου·
> ἀπὸ τότε ἡ βασιλεία τοῦ θεοῦ εὐαγγελίζεται καὶ

πᾶς εἰς αὐτὴν βιάζεται. (Until John, there were the Law and the prophets; since then the good tidings of God's Kingdom are being proclaimed, and everyone is being forced into it.)

At least, if βιάζεται, *biazetai,* is read as having the passive force (as I believe to be correct). And then, of course, there is this:

> 1 Timothy 4:10: . . . ἠλπίκαμεν ἐπὶ θεῷ ζῶντι, ὅς ἐστιν σωτήρ πάντων ἀνθρώπων, μάλιστα πιστῶν. (. . . we have hoped in a living God who is the savior of all human beings, especially those who have faith.)

I could continue, but this might be an auspicious place to pause, at the point of that odd, disorientating final qualification — that μάλιστα, *malista:* "especially." What, after all, could it possibly mean?

For a "hopeful universalist" like Hans Urs von Balthasar, scripture confronts us with something like a dialectical oscillation between two kinds of absolute statements, both indissoluble in themselves and each seemingly irreconcilable with the other. And we are supposedly forbidden — by piety, by doctrine, by prudence — from attempting to decide between them. We can at most juxtapose verses of the sort I have just quoted (along with others of the same sort) with other, more ominous verses that speak of a future discrimination between the righteous and the reprobate, and of an eschatological exclusion or destruction of the wicked. Having done this, supposedly, we must then try prayerfully to hold the two seemingly antinomous sides of scripture's testimony in a sustained "tension," without attempting any sort of final resolution or synthesis between them. In so doing, apparently, we learn to wait on God in a salutary condition of charity toward all and salubrious fear for ourselves—of a joyous certitude regarding the glorious power of God's love and a terrible consciousness of the dreadful might of sin. Perhaps this is the right way of balancing things out, but I am inclined to think not. I see no great virtue in vacillation, especially when it seems like a strategy for crediting oneself with a tenderheartedness that one might nevertheless be willing to doubt in God. This whole posture looks uncomfortably like intellectual timidity to me. Moreover, it seems to encompass just a little too much post-Hegelian dialectical disenchantment, as well perhaps as a touch of disingenuous obscurantism; at least, I cannot quite suppress my suspicion that here the word "tension" is being used merely as an anodyne euphemism for "contradiction." And, frankly, I have no great interest in waiting upon God, to see if in the end he will prove to be better or worse than I might have hoped.

For myself, I prefer a much older, more expansive, perhaps overly systematic approach to the seemingly contrary eschatological expectations unfolded in the New Testament—an approach, that is, like Gregory of Nyssa's or Origen's, according to which the two sides of the New Testament's eschatological language represent not two antithetical possibilities tantalizingly or menacingly dangled before us, posed one against the other as challenges to faith and discernment, but rather two different moments within a seamless narrative, two distinct eschatological horizons, one enclosed within the other. In this way of seeing the matter, one set of images marks the furthest limit of the immanent course of history, and the division therein—right at the threshold between this age and the "Age to come" ('olam ha-ba, in Hebrew)—between those who have surrendered to God's love and those who have not; and the other set refers to that final horizon of all horizons, "beyond all ages," where even those who have traveled as far from God as it is possible to go, through every possible self-imposed hell, will at the last find themselves in the home to which they are called from everlasting, their hearts purged of every last residue of hatred and pride. Each horizon is, of course, absolute within its own sphere: one is the final verdict on the totality of human history, the other the final verdict on the eternal purposes of God—just as the judgment of the cross is a verdict upon the violence and cruelty of human order and human history, and Easter the verdict upon creation as conceived in God's eternal counsels. The eschatological discrimination between heaven and hell is the crucifixion of history, while the final universal restoration of all things is the Easter of creation. This way of seeing the matter certainly seems, at any rate, to make particularly cogent sense of the grand eschatological vision of 1 Corinthians 15. At least, Paul certainly appears to speak there, especially in verses 23–24, of three distinct moments, distributed across two eschatological frames, in the process of the final restoration of the created order in God:

> Ἕκαστος δὲ ἐν τῷ ἰδίῳ τάγματι· ἀπαρχὴ Χριστός, ἔπειτα οἱ τοῦ Χριστοῦ ἐν τῇ παρουσίᾳ αὐτοῦ, εἶτα τὸ τέλος, ὅταν παραδιδῷ τὴν βασιλείαν τῷ θεῷ καὶ πατρί, ὅταν καταργήσῃ πᾶσαν ἀρχὴν καὶ πᾶσαν ἐξουσίαν καὶ δύναμιν. (And each in the proper order: the Anointed as the firstfruits, thereafter those who are in the Anointed at his arrival, then the full completion, when he delivers the Kingdom to him who is God and Father, when he renders every Principality and every Authority and Power ineffectual.)

Only at the very end of these three stages, then—first the exaltation of Christ, then the exaltation at history's end of those already fully united to Christ, and then the "full completion" at the end of all ages, when the Kingdom is yielded over to the Father—do we arrive at the promise of verse 28:

ὅταν δὲ ὑποταγῇ αὐτῷ τὰ πάντα, τότε καὶ αὐτὸς ὁ υἱὸς ὑποταγήσεται τῷ ὑποτάξαντι αὐτῷ τὰ πάντα, ἵνα ᾖ ὁ θεὸς πάντα ἐν πᾶσιν. (And, when all things have been subordinated to him, then will the Son himself also be subordinated to the one who has subordinated all things to him, so that God may be all in all.)

After all, though Paul speaks on more than one occasion of the judgment to come, it seems worth noting that the only picture he actually provides of that final reckoning is the one found in 1 Corinthians 3:11–15, the last two verses of which identify only two classes of the judged: those saved in and through their works, and those saved by way of the fiery destruction of their works.

εἴ τινος τὸ ἔργον μενεῖ ὃ ἐποικοδόμησεν, μισθὸν λήμψεται· εἴ τινος τὸ ἔργον κατακαήσεται, ζημιωθήσεται, αὐτὸς δὲ σωθήσεται, οὕτως δὲ ὡς διὰ πυρός. (If the work that someone has built endures, that one will receive a reward; if anyone's work should be burned away, that one will suffer loss, yet shall be saved, even though as by fire.)

If Paul means us to understand that there will also be yet another class—that of the eternally derelict—he does not say so. And though, admittedly, later tradition has tended to take these verses as referring only to two distinct divisions within the limited company of the elect, Paul certainly says nothing of the sort. If he really believed that the alternative to life in Christ is eternal torment, it seems fairly careless of him to have omitted any mention of the fact. In every instance in which he names the stakes of our relation to Christ, he describes salvation as rescue from death, not from perpetual torture. I know it is traditional to take "death" here as meaning "spiritual death," which really means not death in any obligingly literal and terminal sense, but instead endless agony in separation from God; but Paul would have had to be something of a cretin not to have made that absolutely clear if that was indeed what he intended his readers to understand.

II

I suppose one cannot really discuss New Testament eschatology without considering the book of Revelation. I have to be honest, though: I tend not to think of it as a book about eschatology as such. Admittedly, it is so arcane a text that any absolute pronouncements on its nature or meaning are almost certainly misguided. But, even so, I really do not think one can make sense of it according to any simple division between history and eternity, or between time and time's ending, despite all its extravagant apocalyptic imagery of a world destroyed and restored. In fact, I regard it as a supremely foolish enterprise for anyone to attempt to extract so much as a single clear and unarguable doctrine regarding anything at all from the text (in the way that these days fundamentalist Evangelicals especially like to do, but that Christians of every confession have been wont to do down the centuries). The whole book is to my mind an intricate and impenetrable puzzle, one whose key vanished long ago along with the particular local community of Christians who produced it. The tradition of apocalyptic literature upon which it draws, moreover, is one of such farraginous allegory, and one that consists so thoroughly in the elaborate veiling of political and religious provocations behind fabulous dream-images and esoteric symbolisms and cryptic ciphers, that we delude ourselves if we imagine that—across a distance of two millennia, and without any knowledge of the secretive community from which the text arose, and without any inkling of the cryptadia concealed beneath its countless figural layers—we could hope to grasp even a shadow of a fragment of its intended message. True, the book does contain a few especially piquant pictures of final perdition, if that is what one chooses to cling to as something apparently solid and buoyant amid the whelming floods of all that hallucinatory imagery; but, even then, the damnation those passages describe chiefly falls upon patently allegorical figures like "Hades" (Death personified) or "the Beast" (Rome "brutified"), which hardly seems to allow for much in the way of doctrinal exactitude. As it happens, the text also contains a lamb with seven horns and seven eyes, horses with lions' heads and tails like serpents, giant angels, locusts with iron thoraxes, a dragon with seven heads and ten horns and wearing seven diadems, a great whore seated on the beast and bearing a chalice full of abominations, a gigantic city with streets of transparent gold . . . (and so on and so forth). One would have to be something of a lunatic to mistake any of it for a straightforward statement of dogma.

For myself, for what it is worth, I do not even really think that Revelation is a book about the end of time, so much as a manifesto written in figurative code by a Jewish Christian who

believed in keeping the Law of Moses but who also believed
that Jesus was the Messiah. It is for the most part, as far as I can
tell, an extravagantly allegorical "prophecy" not about the end
of history as such, but about the inauguration of a new historical epoch in which Rome will have fallen, Jerusalem will have
been restored, and the Messiah will have been given power "to
rule the gentiles with a rod of iron." And this new epoch, so
the text clearly seems to announce, will not even really lie beyond history as a continuing reality: There will still, it tells us,
be kings and gentile peoples beyond the walls of God's city,
walking in its light and invited to enter through its open gates.
To me, it is all a religious and political fable, principally concerned with Rome and Judaea in the closing decades of the
first century, and written in extremely obscure symbols for a
community that already understood their hidden meanings.
This is not to deny that it is also of course a vivid testament to a
particular apocalyptic idiom, and so no doubt carries hints and
adumbrations of a larger set of eschatological expectations; but
I see those expectations as mostly accidental to the text's essential message, and find them hazy to the point of unintelligi-
bility. I know that this view of the matter might make the book
considerably less enjoyable for those who think it some kind of
visionary script for the end of time, a magic mirror for scrying
out things yet to come, but I cannot alter my views (since they
are almost certainly correct).

Then again, all things considered, my opinions on the
matter just might spare persons of a more chiliastic bent certain exegetical embarrassments. After all, if one chooses to
read Revelation entirely as a picture of the final judgment of all
creation, and of the great last assize of all souls, one must then
also account for the seeming paradox of a prophesied final
judgment—one that includes a final discrimination between

the saved and the damned—that will nevertheless be succeeded by a new Age in which the gates of the restored Jerusalem will be thrown open, and precisely those who have been
left outside the walls and putatively excluded forever from the
Kingdom will be invited to wash their garments, enter the city,
and drink from the waters of life. I have to say, I could probably accept this as an attractive alternative to my boringly de-
flationary historicizing approach to the text, if I were able to
think of the book as more mystical than political. And perhaps
I should not be so literalist, and should allow for both readings
at once. After all, the curiously extended coda to the book's
scenes of judgment, considered dispassionately, conforms very
well to that notion of two distinct eschatological horizons that
I described above: the more proximate horizon of historical
judgment, where the good and evil in all of us are brought to
light and (by whatever means necessary) separated; and the
more remote horizon of an eternity where a final peace awaits
us all, beyond everything that ever had the power to divide
souls from each other. If John's apocalypse really is about the
end of all things, then it could clearly be taken as promising
two distinct resolutions to fallen time: the end of history in a
final judgment and then, beyond that, the end of judgment in
a final reconciliation. I will, however, leave the matter there.
Again, I do not believe Revelation to be really an eschatological document in anything like the way it has traditionally been
taken, even if I grant that it is cast in shapes provided by some
pre-existing grammar of eschatological hopes and fears; to me
it seems clear that the imaginary landscape traversed by its
garishly figural *dramatis personae* is situated in some liminal
region between history and eternity, political realities and religious dreams.

　　As far as I am concerned, then, those who want to speak

of scriptural prophecy regarding things to come would be well advised not to attempt to make sense of the book of Revelation, in any but the most diffident and tentative way possible, but to inquire instead into the eschatological language used by Christ in the gospels. Here too, admittedly, it seems obvious that those who take the so-called preterist view of much of this language—that is, the view that a great deal of the gospels' talk about a coming tribulation and judgment is most properly understood as referring principally to the fall of Jerusalem and the destruction of the Temple, and therefore to events that are (for us) already long past, even though it is all expressed in the venerable prophetic tropes of a coming epoch of divine wrath and mercy—enjoy an almost unassailable hermeneutical advantage over all other interpreters. If nothing else, the dominical *logia* recorded in Mark (9:1; 13:30) and Matthew (16:28; 24:34) do clearly promise that the "final" tribulations and judgment predicted by Christ will come to pass within the lifetimes of some of his contemporaries, and this apparently caused the evangelists no great embarrassment. And it has been noted often enough by attentive readers that a significant number of Christ's prophecies in the synoptic gospels consist quite literally in jeremiads—that is to say, it is Jeremiah in particular, more than any other of the prophets, whose voice seems at times to be resumed and amplified in the voice of Christ. And just as Jeremiah—specifically in chapters 7, 19, and 31 to 32 of his book—invoked the language of divine judgment and of "the Gehenna" to prophesy the imminent destruction of Jerusalem, followed by its divine restoration and preservation "unto the Age" (31:40), so also Jesus warns in the gospels of a ruin every bit as imminent and as terrible as the one Jeremiah foresaw, also succeeded by a mysterious restoration. One does not even have to believe, as New Testament scholars tend to do, that the most obviously historically situated of these prophecies—the so-called little apocalypse of Mark 13, Matthew 24, and Luke 21—is a specimen of *vaticinium ex eventu* (that is, prognostication written back into the record retrospectively, after the events supposedly foretold have already come to pass). Jesus may indeed have foreseen and foretold it all. Let us assume he did. Even then, in doing so, he nevertheless seems to have been using the cosmic and apocalyptic imagery of transcendent judgment as symbols of a catastrophe immanent to history.

And yet, of course, that cannot be the whole story. The more traditional readings of Christ's prophecies, as direct auguries of the end of history, cannot simply be dismissed. Even if it is the case that many of the prophecies recorded in the synoptic gospels should be understood primarily as spiritual commentaries upon the history of first-century Judaea, expressed in grand and mysterious eschatological figures, by this very token it must also be the case that this same imagery indicates something about the wider eschatological grammar of Christ's teachings as a whole. Moreover, even the most thoroughgoing of preterist readings of the texts cannot obscure the reality that Christ speaks in the gospels not only of a tribulation near at hand for the children of Israel, but also of how the whole of history and the totality of human life stand in light of God's eternity and God's justice. And so one still must ask what Christ promised and what his hearers presumed, concerning both salvation and condemnation. Again, though, this is no easy matter.

Let us consider, to begin with, the very language of heaven and hell, which to us seems so clear, but which is almost impossible to impose consistently or unambiguously upon the Greek of the New Testament. The language of scrip-

ture speaks of a restored creation, of a new Age of the world yet
to dawn, and of a New Jerusalem established upon the earth;
it makes no promises whatsoever about a heaven of redeemed
souls. And, as regards the fate of the derelict, what the actual
text of the New Testament says could scarcely be more evoca-
tively vague. For one thing, there is no single Greek term in
the New Testament that quite corresponds—or corresponds at
all, really—to the Anglo-Saxon word "hell," despite the prodi-
gality with which that term has always been employed in traditional English translations of the text; nor anywhere in scripture do we find a discrete concept that quite corresponds to
the image of hell—a realm of ingenious tortures presided over
by Satan—that took ever more opulent and terrifying mythical shape in later Christian centuries. There is frequent mention of the realm of the dead, Hades, which is generally understood as being located under the earth (or perhaps under the
waters of the seas), and which in Hebrew is called Sheol. This
is where, according to venerable belief, practically all the dead
await the end of time. In Luke, it is there that both the rich
man and Lazarus in Christ's parable are placed, though they
occupy very different regions in its topography. Then there is a
single mention of Tartarus, in verbal form (2 Peter 2:4), a word
borrowed from Greek pagan lore to refer not to a postmortem
destination for souls, but to a place where certain non-human
"spirits"—fallen angels and their demonic offspring the *ne-
filim*—are imprisoned till the end of time (for the curious,
the tales of these unfortunate beings are told in such texts as
1 Enoch and the book of Jubilees, intertestamental writings
that many late antique Jews and Christians regarded as scripture). Finally, there is talk of "the Gehenna," the Greek form
of Ge-Hinnom, "Valley of Hinnom." This is a term that appears eleven times in the synoptic gospels and then only once

more in the New Testament, in the Letter of James. If there is any word in the text that comes near to having something like the meaning we tend to attach to the word "hell" today, this would be it.

Even here, however, we must always keep in mind how immense a cultural and historical chasm separates the world of Jesus of Nazareth from our own. Precisely why the Valley of Hinnom (or, as it was also known, the Valley of Hinnom's Sons) had by Christ's time become a name for a place of judgment, punishment, and purification (usually after death) is difficult to say. It is a real place geographically speaking, as it happens, lying to the south and west of Jerusalem. Its terrain is not particularly inviting, but neither is it particularly infernal. There is an old tradition that it was here that the Tophet—the site of child-sacrifice for worshippers of Moloch and Ba'al, as attested in Leviticus, 2 Chronicles, 2 Kings, Isaiah, and Jeremiah—was located. From well before the Christian period, it was associated with obscene sacrificial practices and evil gods. But, to this point, no significant archaeological find has located a precise place where such things were done. At its southwest boundaries, the valley may also have been a place of Judaean tombs, and perhaps of Roman crematory grounds during the period of occupation, but the evidence to that effect is inconclusive. There is also an uncorroborated tradition from the Middle Ages that says that the valley was used for the disposal and burning of refuse, and perhaps included charnel pits for the disposal of animal and human carrion. If nothing else, this would seem to correspond quite neatly to the description of Hinnom's Valley in Isaiah 66:24 as a site of undying worms and inextinguishable fires (both figures being of course hyperbolic, but also perhaps literal descriptions of the disposal of carrion and refuse). Christ himself borrowed this imagery

(Mark 9:43–48), so perhaps the legend is correct. Then again, one need not necessarily read any of those passages as describing a rubbish tip. The same images are equally consistent with Jeremiah's vision of Hinnom's "valley of slaughter," a place gorged with the corpses of the slain as a result of God's historical punishment of Jerusalem at the hands of Babylon's king, and of Israelites who had worshipped false gods and sacrificed their infants. In the end, though, we really do not know for certain how this valley became a metaphor for divine punishment, in this world or the next. We can only speculate.

Neither do we know with any very great certainty what connotations the term may have had for Jesus or for his listeners in Galilee and Judaea in the early first century. Talk of the Gehenna was part of the common religious parlance of the Jewish world before, during, and soon after the time of Jesus, but how it was interpreted by the differing schools of theology is almost impossible to reduce to a single formula or concept. Clearly it was understood sometimes as a place of final destruction, sometimes simply as a place of punishment, and sometimes as a place of purgatorial regeneration. In both of the two largest and most influential rabbinical schools of Christ's time, those of Shammai and Hillel, it was frequently described as a place of purification or punishment for a finite term; but both schools apparently also taught that there would be some state of final remorse, suffering, or ruin for souls incapable of correction. Shammai is reputed to have been the dourer of the two great rabbis, since he seems to have thought—at least, if the lore has been accurately transmitted and interpreted—that a fairly substantial portion of humanity might ultimately be lost. Even so, for him the Gehenna was principally a place of purification, a refining fire for the souls of those who have been neither incorrigibly wicked nor impeccably good during their lives; and he taught that, once their penance had been completed, those imprisoned there would be released and taken up to paradise. Hillel, by contrast, is reputed to have had considerably greater trust in God's power to save the reprobate from their destruction or damnation, as far as ultimate numbers go; at least, he seemed to think that only a very few might be beyond rescue. But he apparently also thought of the Gehenna as a place of final punishment and annihilation of the bodies and souls of those too depraved to be regenerated. Needless to say, certain of the images employed by Christ to describe the final judgment would have accorded perfectly well with the teachings of either school, though perhaps perfectly with neither. As for what became the dominant view of later rabbinic tradition — that no one can suffer in the Gehenna for more than twelve months — this can be traced back at least to the teachings of Rabbi Akiva (c. 50–135), not long after the time of Christ. It may go back further than that, however. Certainly no one now can say with confidence precisely what Jesus's understanding of the Gehenna's fire was (no matter how adamant the infernalist party may wax in their assertions to the contrary), or what duration he might have assigned to those subjected to it, or even how metaphorically he intended such imagery to be taken. It is obvious that metaphor was his natural idiom as a teacher, and that he employed the prophetic and apocalyptic tropes of his time in a manner more poetic than precise; so it would be foolish to presume that his language of the Valley of Hinnom should be taken any more literally than the imagery of incinerary ovens or seasonal harvests or threshing floors or the closed doors of feasts. Nor does later Christian usage help us much in this matter, given how great a diversity of views the early church accommodated.

So we really cannot know whether Jesus viewed the Ge-

henna's "fire"—itself only an image, surely—as one of annihilation or as one of purification; his metaphors could be interpreted in either way. In support of the former possibility,
one can point to the images of total destruction that Jesus frequently employed, such as dead branches or darnel weeds or
chaff being incinerated in ovens, not to mention his claim that
it lies in God's power to destroy both the body and the soul
in the Gehenna (Matthew 10:28). In support, however, of the
latter possibility—which, incidentally, can explain these seemingly "annihilationist" images equally well—there are those
metaphors used by Jesus that seem to imply that the punishments of the world to come will be of only limited duration:
If remanded to prison, "you shall most certainly not emerge
until you repay the very last pittance" (Matthew 5:26; cf. Luke
12:59); the unmerciful slave is "delivered to the torturers, *until*
he should repay everything he owes" (Matthew 18:34). It seems
as if this "until" should be taken with some seriousness. Some
wicked slaves, moreover, "will be beaten with many blows"
while others will be "beaten with few blows" (Luke 12:49).
I think we can assume that Jesus's listeners were not such pre-
cocious mathematicians that they could foresee the discovery
of greater and lesser infinite sets. And, of course, "*everyone* will
be salted with fire" (Mark 9:49). This fire is explicitly that of
the Gehenna, but salting here is an image of purification and
preservation—for "salt is good" (Mark 9:50). We might even
find some support for the purgatorial view of the Gehenna
from the Greek of Matthew 25:46 (the supposedly conclu-
sive verse on the side of the infernalist orthodoxy), where the
word used for the "punishment" of the last day is κόλασις, *kolasis*—which most properly refers to remedial chastisement—
rather than τιμωρία, *timōria*—which most properly refers to
retributive justice. By the late antique period, admittedly, *ko-*

lasis might have become a word for any sort of legal penalty; the evidence is mixed. But the word's special connotation of corrective rather than retributive punishment was still appreciated and observed by educated writers for centuries after the time of Christ.

Then, of course, one possibility yet remains: that the Gehenna, in Christ's teachings, was a place of neither annihilation nor purification, but rather of eternal conscious torment in a vast torture chamber devised by the God of love (to prove, it seems, the magnitude of that love). To be honest, I see nothing in the gospels that obliges one to believe this. I think, on the whole, that the variety and apparent incompatibility of the metaphors Jesus used to describe the Age to come in his public ministry should be taken as a prohibition upon any dogmatic pronouncements on the matter. I will say, however, that the idea of an eternal punishment for the reprobate—in the sense not merely of a *final* penalty, but also of endlessly perduring torment—seems to have had some substantial precedent in the literature of the intertestamental period, such as 1 Enoch, and perhaps in some early schools of rabbinic thought. But I find no warrant in that for assuming that the highly pictorial and dramatic imagery of exclusion used by Jesus to describe the fate of the derelict when the Kingdom comes—barred or locked doors, the darkness of the night outside the feasting hall, wails of despair and teeth grinding in frustration or anger or misery—corresponds to any particular literal state of affairs, or to some specific perpetual postmortem state of the damned from which there is no hope of deliverance. I am not even willing to presume that the "inexcusable" blasphemy against the Spirit, mentioned in all three synoptic gospels, is one for which an everlasting penalty must be exacted—whether that be endless torment or final annihilation—rather than merely one that necessarily requires purification instead of pardon. The texts of the gospels simply make no obvious claim about a place or state of endless suffering; and, again, the complete absence of any such notion in the Pauline corpus (or, for that matter, in John's gospel, or in the other New Testament epistles, or in the earliest Christian documents of the post-apostolic church, such as the *Didache* and the writings of the "Apostolic Fathers," and so forth) makes the very concept nearly as historically suspect as it is morally repellant. All that can be said with perfect certitude is that to read back into these texts *either* the traditional view of dual eternal postmortem destinies *or* the developed high mediaeval Roman Catholic view of an absolute distinction between "Hell" and "Purgatory" would be either (in the former case) a mere dogmatic reflex or (in the latter) a feat of pure historical illiteracy.

It is hard, I know, to convince most Christians that the picture of hell with which they were raised is not lavishly on display in the pages of scripture. In part, conventional practices of translation—such as the aforementioned custom of using the single English word "hell" as a collective translation for Gehenna, Hades, and Tartarus—are much to blame for this. I have even seen translations that do not follow the established pattern in this regard, mine among them, accused of attempting to expel the traditional picture of hell from the text. But surely translators who have merely rescued distinctions in meaning present in the original Greek can no more be said to have expelled hell from scripture than a workman who oils the hinges on an upstairs door, repairs the window casement around a loose sash, and cuts away the tree branches that scrape against the eaves can be said to have "exorcised" the ghost that the residents of the house had imagined was responsible for all the strange noises keeping them up at night.

Then again, we can grow quite attached to our ghosts. That little thrill of terror they inspire in us when we think we hear them in the sleepless hours before dawn can be positively delectable, at least in retrospect, once the morning has come. Perhaps the thought of hell provides many of us a similar delight, and that is why we are so willing to see it in the text of scripture even where it cannot really be found.

My own view, in the end, is that it is absurd to treat any of the New Testament's eschatological language as containing, even *in nuce,* some sort of exact dogmatic definition of the literal conditions of the world to come. I am quite certain that, while Christ employed all sorts of imagery regarding final judgment, and spoke of a discrimination between the righteous and the wicked, and spoke also of the dire consequences for the latter of their actions in this life, none of it should be received as anything other than an intentionally heterogenous phantasmagory, meant as much to disorient as to instruct. I am quite sure that, had Jesus wished to impart a precise and literal picture of the Age to come, he could have done so. But, in fact, the more closely one looks at the wild mélange of images he employed—especially if one enjoys the luxury of being able to peer down through the strata of conventional translations to the original Greek of the underlying text—the more the picture dissolves into evocation, atmosphere, and poetry. This is only to be expected if we recall the circumstances of Christ's ministry. There was, before all else, a very particular social and (in the broadest sense) political aspect to his language. His condemnations were aimed principally at the rich and powerful, and they expressed his rage against those who exploited and oppressed and ignored the weak, the poor, the ill, the imprisoned. He was a prophet of Israel who, like so many of the prophets of Israel before him, employed the ferocious imagery of a final divine reckoning for creation to denounce the injustices and follies of his age; and, as he was a first-century Jew, the language he used necessarily included much of the terrifying apocalyptic imagery and mythical topographies of Jewish intertestamental literature and early rabbinic teaching. He was telling his contemporaries, and most particularly those among his fellow Jews who had forgotten the justice and the mercy of the Law, that under God's reign it would be the poor and neglected who would be vindicated by divine righteousness, and their oppressors who would be cast down. To me, therefore, it seems almost insane for anyone to imagine that such language can be distilled into specific propositions about heaven and hell, eternity and time, redemption and desolation. All it tells us is that God is just, and that the world he will bring to pass will be one in which mercy has cast out cruelty, and that all of us must ultimately answer for the injustices we perpetrate. It is a language that simultaneously inhabits two distinct ages of the world, two distinct frames of reality, neither of whose terrains or vistas it pretends to describe in literal detail: It at one and the same time announces a justice to be established within historical time by divine intervention and affirms a justice that can be realized only beyond historical time's ultimate conclusion. It is intended, it seems obvious, to move its listeners to both prudent fear and imprudent hope. But, beyond that, only the poetry and the mystery remain.

III

Then too, of course, so many serious exegetical debates coil and roil around the question of whether Christ's teachings about judgment can be said to concern the difference between time and eternity at all, at least as a governing motif, rather than the difference between this age (in Hebrew, '*olam ha-zeh*) and the Age to come ('*olam ha-ba*). Much depends, naturally, on how content one is to see the Greek adjective αἰώνιος, *aiō-nios,* rendered simply and flatly as "eternal" or "everlasting." It is, after all, a word whose ambiguity has been noted since the earliest centuries of the church. Certainly the noun αἰών, *aiōn* (or aeon), from which it is derived, did come during the classical and late antique periods to refer on occasion to a period of endless or at least indeterminate duration; but that was never its most literal acceptation. Throughout the whole of ancient and late antique Greek literature, an "aeon" was most properly an "age," which is simply to say a "substantial period of time" or an "extended interval." At first, it was typically used to indicate the lifespan of a single person, though sometimes it could be used of a considerably shorter period (even, as it happens, a single year). It came over time to mean something like a discrete epoch, or a time far in the past, or an age far off in the future. Plato in the *Timaeus* used it to indicate a kind of time proper to the highest heavenly realm, radically different from sublunary χρόνος, *chronos,* the terrestrial time of generation and decay. He also, incidentally, may have been the first to give the word the adjectival form *aiōnios.* One has to exercise some care even here, however, in making sense of any of these terms in Plato's special usage. It is customary in translations of the *Timaeus* to render the noun *chronos* simply as "time," the noun *aiōn* as "eternity," and the adjective *aiōnios* as "eternal," and credit Plato with the claim therefore that "time is the moving image of eternity"; but these are all, arguably, misleading translations.

For Plato, *chronos* and *aiōn* were not, respectively, time and eternity, but rather two different kinds of time: the former is characterized by change, and therefore consists in that suc-

cessive state of duration (measured out by the sidereal rota-
tions of the heavens) by which things that cannot exist in their
entirety all at once are allowed to unfold their essences through
diachronic extension and through a process of arising and per-
ishing; the latter is characterized by changelessness and reple-
tion, the totality of every essence realized in its fullness in one
immutable state. Thus, the aeon above is the entire "Age" of the
world, existing all at once in a time without movement (which
is to say, change), wherein nothing arises or perishes, while
chronos is the "moving image of the aeon," the dim reflection
of that heavenly plenum in a ghostly procession of shadowy
fragments. Hence, Plato does not really use *aiōnios* to indicate endless duration, because (to employ a slightly later terminology) all duration is a "dynamic" process, a constant passage from possibility to actuality; in the aeon, however, there
is no unrealized *dynamis* or "potency" requiring actualization,
as all exists in a state of immutable fullness, and so nothing
technically "endures" at all. Hence also, for Platonic tradition
as a whole, it may very well be the case that the aeon above is
thought to persist only so long as the present world-cycle endures, and that at the end of the Platonic Year, when the stars
begin their great rotation anew, one heavenly Age will succeed
another. This notion of a changeless heavenly *aiōn* or (in Latin)
aevum, moreover, which stands utterly distinct from the mu-
tability of terrestrial *chronos* or *tempus,* was very much a part
of Christian cosmology from late antiquity well into the late
Middle Ages: here below, the time of generation and decay;
there above, the angelic "age," the ethereal realm of the celestial spheres; and then also, still higher up, the empyrean of
God in himself, "beyond all ages." In a similar but not identical way, *aiōn* also came in ancient usage to mean, as it frequently does in the New Testament, one or another universal

dispensation: this present age of the world, for instance, or the age of the world to come, or a heavenly sphere of reality beyond this world altogether (as it seems to do in John's gospel). On the whole, however, by the time of the New Testament the word's meanings were far too diverse to reduce to any single term now in use in modern languages. Occasionally it could refer to a kind of time, occasionally to a kind of place, occasionally to a particular kind of being or substance, and occasionally to a state of existence. For educated Jewish scholars of Christ's time (or thereabouts) who wrote in Greek, such as Philo of Alexandria (c. 20 BCE–c. 50 CE) and Josephus (37–c. 100), an aeon was still understood as only a limited period of time, often as brief as a single lifespan, occasionally as long as three generations.

Neither did the derivative adjective *aiōnios*—as ἀΐδιος (*aïdios*) or ἀτελεύτητος (*atelevtētos*) did—have the intrinsic meaning of "eternal." It could be used defectively to indicate eternity, in much the way that English words like "enduring" or "abiding" can do today. But it generally had a much vaguer connotation. And the term's plasticity was certainly fully appreciated by the Christian universalists of the Greek and Syrian East in later centuries: Clement, Origen, Gregory of Nyssa, Makrina, Diodore of Tarsus, and so on. As I noted in my introduction, Basil the Great reported that the great majority of his fellow Eastern Christians assumed that the *aiōnios kolasis*, the "chastening of the Age" (or, as it is usually translated in English, "eternal punishment") mentioned in Matthew 25:46, would consist in only a temporary probation of the soul; and he offered no specifically lexicographic objection to such a reading. John Chrysostom (c. 349–407) once even used the word *aiōnios* to describe the reign of Satan over this world precisely in order to emphasize its transience, meaning thereby that Satan's kingdom will last only till the end of the present "age." And, if one is willing to consult the witness of pagan writers—and, after all, the Platonists believed in the torments of "hell" long before the Christians fastened upon the idea— it is worth noting that, as late as the sixth century, the Neo-platonist philosopher Olympiodorus the Younger (c. 495–570) thought it obvious that the suffering of wicked souls in Tar-tarus is certainly not endless, *atelevtos,* but merely very long in duration, *aiōnios.* There were, moreover, regions of the Christian world where such thinking persisted well beyond antiquity. East Syrian tradition remained especially hospitable to the notion of a temporary hell and of God's eventual universal victory over evil. In the thirteenth century, for instance, the East Syrian bishop Solomon of Basra (fl. 1220s and after), in his marvelous *Book of the Bee,* remarked in a quite matter-of-fact manner that in the New Testament *le-alam* or *aiōnios* does not mean "eternal," and that of course hell is not an interminable condition. And the fourteenth-century East Syrian Patriarch Timotheus II (presided 1318–c. 1332) clearly saw it as uncontroversial to assert that hell's *aiōnios* pains will eventually come to an end for everyone, and that the souls cleansed by its fires will enter paradise for eternity.

Admittedly, reflection on the Greek can cast only so much light on the ministry of Christ in Galilee and Judaea. Jesus, according to Luke, was a literate son of the synagogue. This could mean that he was able to read Hebrew or Greek or both (the Jewish Bible of the time, even in the hinterlands of the Galilee, was probably often the most popular Greek version, the Septuagint). Some New Testament scholars and Christian historians down the years have doubted that he was able even to speak Greek fluently, or at all, but I suspect that this is wrong, a hasty conclusion based upon the pronounced tendency of earlier Protestant scriptural scholarship to treat first-century Judaism in the Near East as bizarrely isolated from the larger Graeco-Roman culture in which it had long been immersed. After three centuries of Hellenization, the *lingua franca* of the entire region was *koinē* Greek. Still, nevertheless, we can say with considerable confidence that, when he addressed the multitudes, who were principally the peasantry of Galilee and Judaea, Jesus would certainly have done so in the region's indigenous "vulgar" tongue, Aramaic. And so, if one assumes that the teachings recorded in the gospels are indeed faithful transpositions of the Semitic terms he used into their recognized Greek equivalents, then one must ask precisely which of the former lurk behind the latter in the texts of the New Testament. Here, happily, the Septuagint provides something of a guide. In its pages, the words *aiōn* and *aiōnios* correspond to various forms and uses of the Hebrew *ʿolam* (or *alma* in Aramaic), which can mean an "age," or "epoch," or a time hidden in the far past or far future, or a "world" or "dispensation," or even occasionally perhaps "forever," but which can also mean simply any extended period with a natural term, and not necessarily a particularly long period at that. In Deuteronomy 15:17, for example, where the Hebrew text uses *ʿolam* to indicate the lifespan of a slave, the Greek uses *aiōn*. And, to be honest, there really was no ancient Hebrew term that naturally carried the meaning of "eternity" in a precise sense, understood either as interminable temporal duration or as atemporal changelessness. Rather, Hebrew texts used a number of idiomatic phrases — metaphorical, hyperbolical, periphrastic — by which to convey an impression of extraordinary duration, sometimes so extraordinary as to suggest virtual endlessness. Some of these idioms are visible just below the surface of certain repeated Greek usages in both the Septuagint and the

New Testament. Take, for example, the Greek phrase εἰς τὸν αἰῶνα (*eis ton aiōna*), which is typically rendered into English as "forever," as is correct if one is pedantically precise about the etymological presence of the Latin word *aevum* in the English word "for*ever*," but which might better be rendered today as something like "unto the age" or "for the age." This is the equivalent of the Hebrew *le-olam* or *ad-olam*, whose principal connotation would be something like "from now till the end of this age." Or take the phrases εἰς τοὺς αἰῶνας τῶν αἰώνων (*eis tous aiōnas tōn aiōnōn*) — often translated as "forever and ever," but literally meaning "unto the ages of the ages" — and ὁ αἰὼν τῶν αἰώνων (ʰ*o aiōn tōn aiōnōn*) — "the age of the ages." These are standard Greek correlates of such Hebrew phrases as *le-olam va-ed* ("unto an age and beyond") or *le olamei-olamim* ("unto ages of ages"), which perhaps indicate something like eternity, but which also might be taken as meaning simply an indeterminately vast period of time.

No matter how we interpret the discrete terms, however, we must never forget that today the entire ensemble of references that we bring to these phrases is wholly detached from the religious world of Christ's time, and particularly from its eschatological expectations. It seems absolutely certain, for instance, that the words *aiōn* and *aiōnios* are frequently used in the New Testament as some kind of reference to the ʽ*olam ha-ba*, "the Age to come," which is to say the Age of God's Kingdom, or of that cosmic reality now hidden in God that will be made manifest at history's end. It seems fairly certain, at least, that in the New Testament, and especially in the teachings of Jesus, the adjective *aiōnios* is the equivalent of something like the phrase *le-olam*; and yet it is no less certain that this usage cannot be neatly discriminated from the language of the ʽ*olam ha-ba* without losing something of the special significance it surely possessed in Christ's time. The issue then is not one of *how long,* but rather of *when,* or of *what frame* of reality—what realm, that is, within or beyond history.

IV

Then again, perhaps the issue is in another sense, every bit as essentially, one of origin or nature. In John's gospel, at least, it often seems as if the qualification *aiōnios* indicates neither vast duration nor simply some age that will chronologically succeed the present age, but rather the divine realm of reality that, with Christ, has entered the cosmos "from above." In fact, I tend to think that John's gospel employs the word in a manner not unlike the use Plato made of it in the *Timaeus:* to indicate a supercelestial realm immune to the inconstancy and mortality of the terrestrial realm here below. Whatever the case, however, if one takes the fourth gospel as a kind of second reflection upon the person of Christ, so to speak, a theological commentary on the saving act of God within fallen time, one finds that its language seems irresistibly to point toward a collapse of the distinction between the final judgment of all things and the judgment endured by Christ on Calvary, or between the life of the Age to come and the life that is made immediately present in the risen Christ, or even between Christ's elevation on the cross and his ultimate exaltation as LORD and God over all things. I do not mean that the eschatological horizon of history is erased in the gospel; it is preserved, but is also most definitely in some sense transposed into the here and now, as a divine reality that does not simply follow fallen history, but instead dwells ever above it. John's eschatology is so totally realized in the present, so immanent, that perhaps all that remains of that eschatological horizon within historical

time is the promised cry of Christ that will one day raise the
dead. Then again, perhaps even that too has already sounded
out: "Lazarus, come forth." It is not clear, in any event, that the
fourth gospel foretells any "last judgment" in the sense of a real
additional judgment that accomplishes more than has already
happened in Christ. So perhaps another, still better "preterist"
understanding of Christ's prophecies regarding the coming of
the Son of Adam, one that makes even better sense of his promises to his disciples regarding the Kingdom's imminent advent,
is to see his words as pointing toward and fulfilled within his
own crucifixion and resurrection—wherein all things were
judged, all things redeemed. There is then no longer any scandal in the memory of those dire warnings of imminent judgment that would need explaining away after the fact, and so
there would have been no reason to expunge them from the
record. All that was foretold has indeed already come to pass,
perhaps. The Kingdom has indeed drawn very near, and even
now is being revealed. The hour indeed has come. The "judge
judged in our place" (to use Karl Barth's phrase) is also the resurrection and the life that has always already succeeded and
exceeded the time of condemnation. All of heaven and of hell
meet in those three days—and so now, no matter how far any
soul may venture from God in all the ages, Christ has already
gone further out into that "far country," has borne all the consequences of anyone's alienation from God and neighbor, and
has eternally opened the way back into the sanctuary of the
Presence. In this way, then, the risen Christ truly is himself
already the Temple restored, as his words foretold. And perhaps, then, just as there is a threshold that must yet be crossed
in history between this age and the Age to come, or between
this temporal age here below and that supercelestial Age there
above, so there is also a still more ultimate threshold to be

crossed between that next or higher aeon and the eternal life of God "beyond all ages." After all, as so many biblical scholars have noted, the figure of Christ in the fourth gospel passes through the world as the light of eternity; he is already both judgment and salvation, disclosing hell in our hearts, but shattering it in his flesh, so that he may "drag" everyone to himself. Some things then, perhaps, exist only in being surpassed, overcome, formed, redeemed: "pure nature" (that impossible possibility), "pure nothingness," prime matter, ultimate loss. Hell appears in the shadow of the cross as what has always already been conquered, as what Easter leaves in ruins, to which we may flee from the transfiguring light of God if we so wish, but where we can never finally come to rest—for, being only a shadow, it provides nothing to cling to (as Gregory of Nyssa so acutely observes). Hell exists, so long as it exists, only as the last terrible residue of a fallen creation's enmity to God, the lingering effects of a condition of slavery that God has conquered universally in Christ and will ultimately conquer individually in every soul. This age has passed away already, however long it lingers on in its own aftermath, and thus in the Age to come, and beyond all ages, all shall come home to the Kingdom prepared for them from before the foundation of the world.

Third Meditation
What Is a Person?
A Reflection on the Divine Image

I

I shall begin with a quotation from Pascal's *Pensées,* one that left a mark upon my consciousness the first time I read it many years ago, as an undergraduate:

> Cet écoulement ne nous paraît pas seulement impossible, il nous semble même très injuste; car qu'y a-t-il de plus contraire aux règles de notre misérable justice que de damner éternellement un enfant incapable de volonté, pour un péché où il paraît avoir si peu de part, qu'il est commis six mille ans avant qu'il fût en être? Certainement rien ne nous heurte plus rudement que cette doctrine; et cependant, sans ce mystère, le plus incompréhensible de tous, nous sommes incompréhensible à nous-mêmes. Le nœud de notre condition prend ses replies et ses tours dans cet abîme, de sorte que l'homme est plus inconcevable sans ce mystère que ce mystère

n'est inconcevable à l'homme. (§122 in the current *Pléiade* edition)

(This effluence appears to us not only impossible; it seems indeed very unjust: for what is there more contrary to the rules of our miserable justice than eternally to damn an infant incapable of will, for a sin wherein he appears to have so small a part, as it was committed six thousand years before he was in existence? Certainly nothing offends us more rudely than this doctrine; and yet, without this mystery, the most incomprehensible of all, we are incomprehensible to ourselves. The knot of our condition takes its twists and turns in this abyss, in such a way that man is more inconceivable without this mystery than this mystery is inconceivable to man.)

This is, as it happens, entirely backwards. Generally speaking, there is something deeply attractive in Pascal's cosmic despair—the pervasive plangency of its melancholy, its occasional ghastly sublimities, its dreamlike vagrancies amid the vastitudes of a suddenly unfamiliar universe—but, whenever one catches a glimpse of the specific doctrinal commitments sustaining that despair, the picture begins to lose its enchanting pathos and to become instead something noisome, morbid, even a bit diabolical. For me, this passage is an exquisite specimen of the way in which Christians down the centuries (and, I like to think, Western Christians with a special genius) have excelled at converting the "good tidings" of God's love in Christ into something dreadful, irrational, and morally horrid.

Admittedly, it is difficult not to admire the sheer ingenuity with which, having arrived at dogmatic commitments that no conscience not cowed by terror could abide, many of them have striven to make the abominable seem, if not palatable, at least vaguely reasonable. They have beguiled themselves with those curious fables I have already mentioned above: they tell themselves, say, that an eternity of torment is an entirely condign penalty for even the smallest imaginable sin, the most trivial peccadillo, the pettiest lapse of plain morality, because the gravity of any transgression must be measured by the dignity of the one whom it has wronged, and God necessarily possesses infinite dignity; or they tell themselves that the revelation of God's sovereign glory, in dereliction and redemption, is a good surpassing every other, so good indeed as to make the perpetual sufferings of rational beings somehow a happy circumstance in the optics of eternity. But again, of course, all of this is nonsense: guilt's "proportion" is not an objective quantity, but an evaluation, and only a monstrous justice would refuse to assign guilt according to the capacities and knowledge of the transgressor; and a glory revealed by cruelty or vengeance is no glory at all. Whatever Christians have told themselves to make sense of this teaching, however, the one thing they have always had scrupulously to avoid thinking about deeply is what the character of God would have to be for him to have been willing to create a world of finite spirits on such terms as these. But I have made that point already at some length. So, suffice it here to say that there are moments when I find it difficult not to think that Christianity's chief distinction among theistic creeds is that it alone openly enjoins its adherents to be morally superior to the God they worship.

I suspect that no figure in Christian history has suffered a greater injustice as a result of the desperate inventiveness of the Christian moral imagination than the Apostle Paul, since it was the violent misprision of his theology of grace—starting with the great Augustine, it grieves me to say—that gave rise to almost all of these grim distortions of the gospel. Aboriginal guilt, predestination *ante praevisa merita,* the eternal damnation of unbaptized infants, the real existence of "vessels of wrath," and so on—all of these odious and incoherent dogmatic *leitmotifs,* so to speak, and others equally nasty, have been ascribed to Paul. And yet each and every one of them not only is incompatible with the guiding themes of Paul's proclamation of Christ's triumph and of God's purpose in election, but is something like their perfect inversion. Consider, for instance, the ninth through the eleventh chapters of Romans, which for Augustinian tradition provide the *locus classicus* of its theology of "grace." From very early on in Western Christian history, these admittedly complex but hardly hermetic pages came to be misread in two crucial ways: firstly, as an argument regarding the eternal discrete destinies of individual souls rather than as a contemplation of the relation between Jews and Christians within the covenant; and, secondly, as a collection of declamatory statements rather than as a continuous discourse upon a single, explicitly hypothetical question. And the result was something atrocious.

This is all fairly odd, really. Paul's argument in those chapters is not difficult to follow, at least so long as one does not begin from defective premises. What preoccupies him from beginning to end is the agonizing mystery that (so he believes) the Messiah of Israel has come and yet so few of the children of the house of Israel have accepted the fact, even while so many from outside the covenant have. What then of God's faithfulness to his promises? How can the promised Messiah of Israel fail to be the savior of, quite specifically, Israel? Paul's is not an abstract question regarding which individual human beings are the "saved" and which the "damned." In fact, by the end of the argument, the former category proves to be vastly larger than that of the "elect" or the "called," while the latter category makes no appearance at all. His is a much more general question concerning the two communities of Israel and of the church, and the answer at which he ultimately arrives is one that he draws ingeniously from the logic of election in Jewish scripture. He begins his reflections, it is true, by limning the problem that torments him in the starkest terms imaginable; but he does so in a completely and explicitly conditional voice. We know, he says, that divine election is God's work alone, not earned but given; it is not by their merit that gentile believers have been chosen. "Jacob have I loved, but Esau have I hated" (9:13) (though here, recall, Paul is quoting Malachi, for whom Jacob symbolizes Israel and Esau symbolizes Edom, which would seem to be, if one imagines the point to be merely the separation between the damned and the saved, the very inverse of the typology Paul is employing). For his own ends, Paul continues, God hardened Pharaoh's heart. He has mercy on whom he will, hardens whom he will (9:15–18). And if you think this unjust, who then are you, O man, to reproach the God who made you? May not the potter cast his clay for purposes both high and low, as he chooses (9:19–21)? So, "then, *what if*" (εἰ δέ, *ei de*) God should show his power by preserving vessels suitable only for wrath, keeping them solely for destruction, in order to provide an instructive counterpoint to the riches of the glory he lavishes on vessels prepared for mercy, whom he has called from among the Jews and the gentiles alike (9:22–24)? It is a terrible possibility, admittedly, and horrifying to contemplate, but perhaps that is simply how things are: The elect alone are to be saved, and the rest left reprobate, solely as a display of divine might; God's faithfulness is his own affair. Well then, so far, so Augustinian. But then also, again, so purely conditional: that "what if . . . ?" must be strictly observed. For, as it happens, rather than offering a solution to the quandary in which he finds himself, Paul is simply restating that quandary in its bleakest possible form, at the very brink of despair. He does not stop there, however, because he knows that this cannot be the correct answer. It is so obviously preposterous, in fact, that a wholly different solution must be sought, one that makes sense and that will not require the surrender either of Paul's reason or of his confidence in God's righteousness. Hence, contrary to his own warnings, Paul does indeed continue to question God's justice; and he spends the next two chapters unambiguously rejecting the provisional answer (the "vessels of wrath" hypothesis) altogether, so as to reach a completely different—and far more glorious—conclusion. And, again, his reasoning is based entirely upon the language of election in Jewish scripture.

Throughout the book of Genesis, that is to say, the pattern of God's election is persistently, even perversely antinomian: Ever and again, the elder to whom the birthright properly belongs is supplanted by the younger, whom God has chosen in defiance of all natural "justice." This is practically the running motif uniting the whole text, from Cain and Abel to Manasseh and Ephraim. But—and this is crucial—that pattern is one not of exclusion and inclusion, but rather of a providential delay and divagation in the course of the natural "justice" of primogeniture, as a result of which the scope of election has time to be immensely widened, so that ultimately it takes in not only the brother originally and "justly" excluded by the law of primogeniture (Jacob, for example), but also the brother (Esau, for instance) who had been "unjustly" pretermitted by God's subversion of custom. There is, it turns out, no final division between the elect and the derelict here at all, but rather the precise opposite: the final embrace of all parties in the single and inventively universal grace of election. This is why Esau and Jacob provide so apt a typology for Paul's argument. Esau, we must remember, is not finally rejected in the story of the two brothers; he and Jacob are reconciled, to the increase of both, precisely as a consequence of their temporary estrangement. Indeed, when they are reunited, it is Jacob who says to Esau (not the reverse), "Seeing your face is like seeing God's." And this is the pattern Paul explicitly invokes in his argument. In the case of Israel and the church, moreover, election has become even more literally "antinomian": Christ is the end of the Law (in the sense both of its purpose and of its conclusion) and for precisely this reason all persons may attain righteousness; with the fulfillment of the Law's righteousness, its prescriptions and restrictions have been set aside, the wall of separation between peoples has been removed, and any difference between Jew and gentile has been effaced; thus God blesses everyone (10:11–12). As for the believing "remnant" of Israel (11:5), it turns out that they have been elected not as the limited number of the "saved" within Israel, but as the earnest through which *all* of Israel will be saved (11:26); they are the part that makes the totality holy (11:16). And, again, as was continually the case in Genesis, the providential ellipticality of election's course vastly enlarges its embrace: For the time being, true, a part of Israel is hardened, but this will remain the case only until the "full entirety" (πλήρωμα, *plērōma*) of the gentiles enter in. The unbelievers among the children of Israel may have been allowed to stumble, but God will never allow them to fall. And so, if their failure now brings enrichment to the world, how much more will they provide when

their own "full entirety" (*plērōma*) enter in? Temporarily excluded (like Esau) for the sake of "the world's reconciliation,"
they too will at the last be restored to God's grace; and this will
be nothing less than a "resurrection from the dead" (11:11–12,
15). This, then, is the radiant answer dispelling the shadows of
Paul's grim "what if" in the ninth chapter of Romans, its clar-
ion negative. It turns out that there is no final illustrative division between vessels of wrath and vessels of mercy; that was
a grotesque, all-too-human thought that can now be chased
away for good. God's wisdom far surpasses ours, and his love
can accomplish all that it intends. He has bound everyone in
disobedience so as to show mercy to everyone (11:32): *all* are
vessels of wrath precisely so that *all* may be made vessels of
mercy. As I say, not a difficult argument to follow, if one has
the will to do so.

Not that one can ever, apparently, be explicit enough.
One classic construal of those glorious closing reflections in
the eleventh chapter of Romans, particularly in the Reformed
tradition, is to claim that Paul's seemingly extravagant language—"all," "full entirety," "the world," and so on—really still
means no more than that all peoples will be saved only in the
"exemplary" or "representative" form of the tiny number of
the elect. But this is absurd, of course. Paul is utterly and un-
waveringly clear that it is precisely those *not* called forth, those
who are not the "elect," those who have instead been allowed to
stumble, who still will never be allowed to fall. Those whom he
identifies as "elect" do not constitute the whole number of the
saved; they are merely the firstfruits of the grand plan of salvation. The "derelict" too will, at the close of the tale, be gathered
in, caught up in the embrace of election before they can strike
the ground. And this is, of course, the only conclusion that
can deliver Paul from his fears. If he were not able to reach

it, and not able to argue it through to his own satisfaction, he would end his contemplations in the same darkness in which he began, his glorious discovery would be reduced to a dreary tautology, and his magnificent vision of divine love's vast reach would be converted into a ludicrous cartoon of its squalid narrowness. Yet, on the whole, the late Augustinian tradition on these texts has been so broad and mighty that it has, for millions of Christians, effectively evacuated Paul's argument of all its real content. It ultimately made possible those spasms of theological and moral nihilism that prompted Calvin, as I have noted, to claim that God predestined even the fall of humanity, and that he hates the reprobate. *Sic transit gloria Evangelii.* This is perhaps the most depressing paradox ever to have arisen in the whole Christian theological tradition: that Paul's great attempt to demonstrate that God's election is not some arbitrary act of predilective exclusion, but instead a providential means for bringing about the unrestricted inclusion of all persons, has been employed for centuries to advance what is quite literally the very teaching that he went to such great lengths explicitly to reject.

II

So it goes. Even Homer nods. And Augustine, for all his brilliance, did quite a lot of nodding in his later years. Would that Christian tradition had—this is my incessant lament, my tireless refrain, my *cri de cœur*—heeded Gregory of Nyssa instead. So many unpleasant confusions might have been avoided, so many young minds might have been preserved against psychological abuse, so many Christian moral imaginations might have been spared such enormous corruptions. When Gregory looked at the eschatological language of the New Testament, what he believed he saw was—as I said in my First Meditation—not some everlasting division between the two cities of the redeemed and the reprobate, but only a provisional division between two moments within the single economy of a universal salvation. What he found was—as I phrased it in my Second Meditation—two distinct eschatological horizons, one wholly enclosed within the other. For him, the making and redemption of the world belong to that one great process by which God brings to pass the perfect creation that has resided from everlasting in the divine will, conceived and intended by him before all ages. All of created time is, he believed, nothing but the gradual unfolding, in time and by way of change, of God's eternal and immutable design. For him, in fact, creation is twofold; there is a prior (which is to say, eternal) creative act that abides in God, as the end toward which all things are directed and for the sake of which all things have been brought about (described in Genesis 1:1–2:3); and there is a posterior creative act, which is the temporal exposition—cosmic and historical—of this divine model (whose initial phases are described in Genesis 2:4–25). From eternity, says Gregory, God has conceived of humanity under the form of an ideal "Human Being" (ἄνθρωπος, anthrōpos), at once humanity's archetype and perfection, a creature shaped entirely after the divine likeness, neither male nor female, possessed of divine virtues: purity, love, impassibility, happiness, wisdom, freedom, and immortality. But this does not mean, as we might expect, simply that God first created the eternal ideal of the human, and only then fashioned individual human beings in imitation of this universal archetype. Rather, for Gregory, this primordial "ideal" Human Being comprises—indeed, is identical with—the entire plērōma of all human beings in every age, from first to last. In his great treatise On the Making of

Humanity, Gregory reads Genesis 1:26–7 — the first account of
the creation of the race, where humanity is described as being
made "in God's image" — as referring not to the making of
Adam as such, but to the conception within the eternal divine
counsels of this full community of all of humanity: the whole
of the race, comprehended by God's "foresight" as "in a single
body," which only in its totality truly reflects the divine likeness and the divine beauty. As for the two individuals Adam
and Eve, whose making is described in the second creation
narrative, they may have been superlatively endowed with
the gifts of grace at their origin, but they were themselves still
merely the first members of that concrete community that only
as a whole can truly reflect the glory of its creator. For now, it is
only in the purity of the divine wisdom that this human totality
subsists "altogether" (ἀθρόως, *athroōs*) in its own fullness. It
will emerge into historical actuality, in the concrete fullness
of its beauty, only at the end of a long temporal "unfolding" or
"succession" (ἀκολουθία, *akolouthia*). Only then, when time
and times are done, will a truly redeemed humanity, one that
has passed beyond all ages, be recapitulated in Christ. Only
then also, in the ultimate solidarity of all humankind, will a
being made in the image and likeness of God have truly been
created: "Thus 'Humanity according to the image' came into
being," writes Gregory, "the entire nature [or race], the Godlike
thing. And what thus came into being was, through omnipotent wisdom, not part of the whole, but the entire plenitude of
the nature altogether." It is precisely and solely this full community of persons throughout time that God has elected as his
image, truth, glory, and delight. And God will bring this good
creation he desires to pass in spite of sin, both within human
history and yet over against it. He will never cease to bring the
story he intends in creation to pass, despite our apostasy from

that story. At the same time, however—so Gregory says in his treatise *On Virginity*—sin has inaugurated its own history, its own *akolouthia* of privation and violence, spreading throughout time from its own first seeds, striving against God's love. And so, of course, throughout the course of human history, God's original unfolding of creation must overcome the parasitic unfolding of evil. Even so, humanity, understood as the *plērōma* of God's election, never ceases to possess that deathless beauty that humanity, understood as an historical community, has largely lost. God, reflecting eternally upon that beauty, draws all things on toward the glory he intends for them, although according to a mystery—a grace that does not predetermine the operations of a human freedom that, nevertheless, cannot ultimately elude it.

For Gregory, moreover, this human totality belongs to Christ from eternity, and can never be alienated from him. According to *On the Making of Humanity*, that eternal Human Being who lives in God's counsels was from the first fashioned after the beauty of the Father's eternal Logos, the eternal Son, and was made for no other end than to become the living body of Christ, who is its only head. It is thus very much the case that, for Gregory, the whole drama of Christ's incarnation, death, and resurrection was undertaken so that the eternal Son might reclaim those who are his own—which is to say, everyone. By himself entering into the plenitude of humanity as a single man among other men and women, and in thereby assuming humanity's creaturely finitude and history as his own, Christ reoriented humanity again toward its true end; and, because the human totality is a living unity, the incarnation of the Logos is of effect for the whole. In a short commentary on the language of the eschatological "subordination" of the Son to the Father in the fifteenth chapter of 1 Corinthians, Gregory

even speaks of Christ as having assumed not just human nature in the abstract, but the whole *plērōma*, which means that
his glory has entered into all that is human. Nor could it be
otherwise. Such is the indivisible solidarity of humanity, he
argues, that the entire body must ultimately be in unity with
its head, whether that be the first or the last Adam. Hence
Christ's obedience to the Father even unto death will be made
complete only eschatologically, when the whole race, gathered
together in him, will be yielded up as one body to the Father, in
the Son's gift of subjection, and God will be all in all. At Easter,
Christ's resurrection inaugurated an *akolouthia* of resurrection, so to speak, in the one body of the race, an unfolding that
cannot now cease (given the unity of human nature) until the
last residue of sin—the last shadow of death—has vanished.
Gregory finds this confirmed also, according to one of his early
treatises (a "Refutation" of the teachings of the theologian
Eunomius), in John 20:17: When Christ, says Gregory, goes
to his God and Father, to the God and Father of his disciples,
he presents all of humanity to God in himself. In his *On the
Soul and Resurrection,* moreover, Gregory reports the teaching
of his sister Makrina that, when this is accomplished, all divisions will at last fall away, and there will no longer be any separation between those who dwell within the Temple precincts
and those who have been kept outside, for every barrier of sin
separating human beings from the mysteries within the veil of
the sanctuary will have been torn down; and then there will be
a universal feast around God in which no rational creature will
be deprived of full participation, and all those who were once
excluded on account of sin will enter into the company of the
blessed. We see here the exquisite symmetry in Gregory's reading of scripture's narrative of creation and redemption, and in
his understanding of eternity's perfect embrace of history: just

as the true first creation of humanity (Genesis 1:26–27) was the eternal conception in the divine counsels of the whole race united to him while the second (Genesis 2:7) was the inauguration of a history wholly dependent upon that eternal decree, so the culmination of history (1 Corinthians 15:23) will at the last be, as it were, succeeded by and taken up into this original eternity in its eschatological realization (1 Corinthians 15:24), and the will of God will be perfectly accomplished in the everlasting body of Christ.

For Gregory, then, there can be no true human unity, nor even any perfect unity between God and humanity, except in terms of the concrete solidarity of all persons in that complete community that is, alone, the true image of God. God shall be all in all, argues Gregory in a treatise on infants who die prematurely, not simply by comprising humanity in himself in the abstract, as the universal ideal that he redeems in a few select souls, but by joining each particular person, each unique inflection of the *plērōma*'s beauty, to himself. Even so, Christ's assumption and final recapitulation of the human cannot simply be imposed upon the race as a whole, but must effect the conversion of each soul within itself, so that room is truly made for God "in all"; salvation by union with Christ must unfold within human freedom, and so within our capacity to venture away. For Gregory, of course, good classical Christian metaphysician that he was, evil and sin are always accidental conditions of human nature, never intrinsic qualities; all evil is a privation of an original goodness, and so the sinfulness that separates rational creatures from God is only a disease corrupting and disabling the will, robbing it of its true rational freedom, and thus is a disorder that must ultimately be purged from human nature in its entirety, even if needs be by hell. As Gregory argues in *On the Making of Humanity,* evil is inher-

ently finite—in fact, in a sense, is pure finitude, pure limit—
and so builds only toward an ending; evil is a tale that can
have only an immanent conclusion; and, in the light of God's
infinity, its proper end will be shown to be nothing but its
own disappearance. Once it has been exhausted, when every
shadow of wickedness—all chaos, duplicity, and violence—
has been outstripped by the infinity of God's splendor, beauty,
radiance, and delight, God's glory will shine in each creature
like the sun in an immaculate mirror, and each soul—born
into the freedom of God's image—will turn of its own nature
toward divine love. There is no other place, no other liberty; at
the last, to the inevitable God humanity is bound by its freedom. And each person, as God elects him or her from before
the ages, is indispensable, for the humanity God eternally wills
could never come to fruition in the absence of any member of
that body, any facet of that beauty. Apart from the one who is
lost, humanity as God wills it could never be complete, nor
even exist as the creature fashioned after the divine image; the
loss of even one would leave the body of the Logos incomplete,
and God's purpose in creation unaccomplished.

III

Really, we should probably already know all of this—not for
theological reasons, but simply from a sober consideration of
any truly coherent account of what it means to be a person.
After all, it would be possible for us to be saved as individuals
only if it were possible for us to be persons as individuals; and
we know we cannot be. And this, in itself, creates any number
of problems for the majority view of heaven and hell. I am not
even sure that it is really possible to distinguish a single soul
in isolation as either saint or sinner in any absolute sense, in-

asmuch as we are all bound in disobedience (as the Apostle says) precisely by being bound to one another in the sheer contingency of our shared brokenness, and the brokenness of our world, and our responsibility one for another. Consequently, I cannot even say where—at what extremity of pious despair—I could possibly draw a line of demarcation between tolerable and intolerable tales of eternal damnation. Some stories, of course, are obviously too depraved to be credited and may be rejected out of hand: A child who, for instance, is born one day in poverty, close to the sun in lonely lands, suffers from some horrible and quite incurable congenital disease, dies in agony, unbaptized, and then—on some accounts, consecrated by theological tradition—descends to perpetual torment as the just penalty for a guilt inherited from a distant ancestor, or as an epitome of divine sovereignty in election and dereliction, or whatever. Now most of us will recognize this to be a degenerate parody of the gospel, so repugnant to both reason and conscience that—even were it *per impossibile* true—it would be morally indefensible to believe it. But, then, under what conditions precisely, and at what juncture, does the language of eternal damnation really cease to be scandalous? For me, it never does, and for very simple reasons. Let us presume that that child who dies before reaching the font does not in fact descend into hell, and is not even conveniently wafted away on pearl-pale clouds of divine tenderness into the perfumed limbo of unbaptized babes, but instead (as Gregory of Nyssa believed such a child would do) ascends to eternal bliss, there to grow forever into a deeper communion with God. This is a much cheerier picture of things, I think we can all agree. But let us not stop there. Let us go on to imagine also another child born on the same day, this one in perfect health, who grows into a man of monstrous temperament, cruel, selfish, even

murderous, and who eventually dies unrepentant and there-
upon descends to an endless hell. Well, no doubt this brute
chose to become what he became, to the extent that he was able
to do so, conscious of the choices he was making; so maybe he
has received no more than he deserves. And yet, even then,
I cannot quite forget, or consider it utterly irrelevant, that he
was born into a world so thoroughly ruined that a child can
be born one day in poverty, suffer from some horrible and incurable congenital disease, die in agony . . . What precisely did
that wicked man, then, ever really know of the Good? And
how clearly, and with what rational power over his own will?
Certainly he did not know everything, at least not with perfect clarity, nor did he enjoy complete rational discretion or
power over his own deeds and desires. Not even a god would
be capable of that. This thought alone is enough to convince
me of the sheer moral squalor of the traditional doctrine.

Yet this still is not my principal point. I want to say something far more radical, something that I touched upon lightly
in my First Meditation above. I want to say that there is no
way in which persons can be saved *as persons* except in and
with all other persons. This may seem an exorbitant claim,
but I regard it as no more than an acknowledgment of certain obvious truths about the fragility, dependency, and exi-
gency of all that makes us who and what we are. I assume, or
at least hope, that none of us is able to agree with the argument of Thomas (among others) that the knowledge of the torments of the damned will increase the felicity of the blessed in
heaven (see *Summa Theologiae,* supplement to the third part,
qu. 94)—even if, as the more irrepressibly eager of Thomas's
apologists will always helpfully observe, he means only that
the saints will derive pleasure from the contrast between their
beatitude and the damnation from which they were graciously

spared, and not that the blessed will take sadistic delight in the spectacle as such. Needless to say, this is a meaningless distinction, since the ability to find pleasure in seeing another suffering pains to which one is oneself immune is in fact what sadism is. But why debate the point? Most of us today are not going to defend the argument, no matter how it is qualified. We simply lack the phlegm of a mediaeval Italian noble, living in an age when torture and dungeons and summary execution for minor offenses were inextricably woven into the coarse fabric of life. Our tenderer consciences today require somewhat more emollient formulations. As it turns out, however, this is nowhere near as simple a matter as one might imagine. Many of today's gentler infernalists, in their efforts to make emotional sense of the idea of a heaven forever suspended above hell's abyss, and of a paradise in which the bliss of the saints is undiminished by the misery of those they left behind, end up making proposals scarcely any less chilling. I recently read an Evangelical apologist for the infernalist orthodoxies argue that it is morally correct for the saved to cease from pity for the damned simply because such pity is fruitless, just as it is forgivable to avert one's eyes from a frightful accident on the roads from which one cannot rescue the victims, and to cease to think about it entirely. This, it should be needless to say, is nothing more than a counsel of moral imbecility. Neither can my pity for a little girl dying of cancer cure her, for what that is worth; but what an atrocity of a man I would be if I ceased pitying her for that reason.

Perhaps, though, I am illicitly tipping the scales here by choosing an example so fraught with bathos. Maybe there are more pardonable forms of indifference to the sufferings of others. At least, one Catholic philosopher recently reproached me online for exaggerating the scandal in the traditional proposal that the saints in heaven will not be bothered in the least (as of course they could not be) about the torments of the damned below. After all, he argued, few of us ever spare a thought for, say, the serial murderer incarcerated for life, also out of sight and out of mind, a castaway on one or another island of misery in the archipelago of America's brutal penitentiary system. There is certainly nothing at all culpable in our apathy here, he claimed. I should note first that I am not entirely sure how to answer such an argument, because it strikes me as so profoundly unchristian as to call into question this philosopher's entire understanding of the faith. Certainly the closing verses of Matthew's twenty-fifth chapter seem to suggest that Christians are held to a very different standard of ethical concern. But, more to the point, my critic was reducing the issue to one of individual psychological engagement, a private concern for the fate of one or another individual miscreant. True, most of us do not spare a thought for the murderer in prison—though, frankly, there is nothing particularly commendable in that dreary emotional fact, nor is it a good guide to how we should expect to see things from the perspective of eternity, free from sin and selfishness—but it is also true that that murderer's brother, mother, father, sister, child, wife, or friend *must* think about him, and *must* suffer grief at the thought of what he has become and the end he has reached. This means, I submit, that our indifference to his fate must also logically be an indifference to their sufferings as well. And it requires little imagination to see how this small, prudent, seemingly rational degree of callousness on our part might be magnified, if carried into the calculus of eternity, into an absolute moral detachment from all other persons. After all, taken to its most extreme logical entailments, our willingness to surrender even the most depraved of souls to a final unrelieved torment

is, tacitly, a willingness also to ignore the sufferings of potentially everyone. And, as I have noted above, what one is willing
to sacrifice to achieve a certain end, even if only potentially, is
a price that, morally speaking, one has already paid, whether
or not the actual eventuality of that sacrifice should ever arise.
We cannot choose to cease to care for *any* soul without thereby
choosing to cease to care for *every* soul to which that particular soul is attached by bonds of love or loyalty, and for every
other soul attached to each of these, and, if need be, for every
soul that has ever been — if that is what it takes to be perfectly,
blissfully indifferent to the damned. No soul is who or what it
is in isolation; and no soul's sufferings can be ignored without
the sufferings of a potentially limitless number of other souls
being ignored as well. And so, it seems, if we allow the possibility that even so much as a single soul might slip away un-
mourned into everlasting misery, the ethos of heaven turns out
to be "every soul for itself" — which is also, curiously enough,
precisely the ethos of hell.

I know of another Evangelical writer — this one a philosopher (of sorts) who periodically insists on perpetrating
theology, always with catastrophic results — who is wholly
committed to the infernalist orthodoxy, but who at least has
the instinctive decency to recognize that indifference is not
sufficiently distinct from malice to count as a genuine moral
stance. And apparently he also grasps that talk of a final beatitude that might involve specifically averting one's thoughts
from certain persons one has loved in the past is, at the very
least, counterintuitive. He therefore proposes just the opposite
of the Thomistic picture: not that God, in order to increase the
felicity of the blessed, will provide them with the delectable
diversion of watching the damned writhing amid the fire and
brimstone, but that instead, in order to grant them the per-

fect blessedness of the Kingdom, he will veil the sufferings of
the damned from their eyes, and will even elide all memory of
the lost from their recollections. Think of it as a kind of heavenly lobotomy, a small, judicious mutilation of the intellect,
the surrender of a piece of the mind in exchange for peace of
mind. After all, consider how happy we could all be if we never
had to think of anyone's sufferings at all. I suppose that this
is better than the Thomistic picture; it demonstrates a keener
sense of charity, at least; but it is charity of a distinctly tragic
variety, I have to say. How terrible to imagine that the beatitude of the saints must consist to some degree in the destruction of part of their humanity. And surely a blessedness that
subsists only by way of ignorance is one of a peculiarly defective kind. But perhaps these really are the only alternatives the
infernalist has to choose among: If there really is an eternal
hell, where souls suffer in perpetuity, perhaps the blessedness
of the saved absolutely must in some large measure consist
either in callousness or in ignorance. If so, the latter is the less
appalling of two quite appalling options.

Now, granted, part of the absurdity of such arguments
is the mundane psychologization of heaven and hell they involve, and the somewhat burlesque effects produced whenever one attempts to imagine the unimaginable in terms of the
familiar. Whatever the world to come may be, it surely will
not involve the souls of the saved gathering like eager tourists
along steel railings above the Grand Canyon, gazing down into
hell and waving impishly to their aunts and cousins among the
flames. But, that aside, there remains a far larger and grimmer
absurdity in the moral possibilities these arguments ask us to
entertain, and what those possibilities imply about the meaning of any human love. Needless to say, we cannot describe, or
even faintly imagine, what the final state of a redeemed soul

might be like. But Christians are obliged, it seems clear, to take seriously the eschatological imagery of scripture; and there all talk of salvation involves the promise of a corporate beatitude—a Kingdom of love and knowledge, a wedding feast, a city of the redeemed, the body of Christ—which means that the hope Christians cherish must in some way involve the preservation of whatever is deepest in and most essential to personality, rather than a perfect escape from personality. But finite persons are not self-enclosed individual substances; they are dynamic events of relation to what is other than themselves. And this poses a problem. For me, all attempts to imagine the conditions of God's Kingdom over against the reality of the eternal torment of those outside its demesne irresistibly summon up a single recurrent image: that of a parent whose beloved child has grown into quite an evil person, but who remains a parent nevertheless and therefore keeps and cherishes countless tender memories of the innocent and delightful being that has now become lost in the labyrinth of that damaged soul. Is all of that—those memories, those anxieties and delights, those feelings of desperate love—really to be consigned to the fire, as just so much combustible chaff? Must it all be forgotten, or willfully ignored, for heaven to enter into that parent's soul? And, if so, is this not the darkest tragedy ever composed, and is God not then a tragedian utterly merciless in his poetic omnipotence? Moreover, who then exactly is that parent when he or she has achieved union with God, once those memories have been either converted into indifference or altogether expunged? Who or what is that being whose identity is no longer determined by its relation to that child? I cannot help but feel that this is something like the paradox of the ship of Theseus, except that in this case—in which the deepest emotional and personal elements that compose a soul have been stripped away—it is the living form, rather than its mere material instantiation, that has been obliterated. So why would we even speak about salvation at that point, rather than about the total replacement of one thing by another? Who is it, after all, who remains to be saved? A spark, a spiritual essence detached from all identity, rather like the Western caricature of *advaita Vedanta*'s eternal *Atman* detached from the conditional relations of the *jiva*? Is the bliss of the beatific union with God so transfiguring and consuming and complete as to reduce all subsidiary relations to nothing, and thereby in a single stroke to reduce each personhood to nothing, so that all that remains is an anonymous act of intellection immersed in perpetual, unpitying delight? This is an obvious thing, really: This blessedly "oblivious" account of the afterlife of the elect is incoherent simply because, for salvation to be the salvation of persons—as opposed to the final liberation of something anonymous and "transcendent" of personality, something that must be rescued from its defiling entanglement in personality's pathetic need for others—there must be some sort of continuity of identity between the soul as it exists during its wanderings in this vale of tears and the soul as it shall be when it is raised up into God. And such continuity is impossible apart from those we love, because we are, as persons, the creatures of our loves.

At this point, I have to admit, I find myself irresistibly calling to mind what I feel fairly certain is a cliché of crime fiction or melodrama or even comedy (at least, I seem to remember a William Powell and Myrna Loy film based on the premise): that of the long-term amnesiac who has made a good life for himself, and even raised a family, but who then discovers he may have committed crimes in his previous life, and now must determine whether in fact he did, and whether, should it prove so, he is still the man who was guilty of those earlier deeds. The issue here, however, is a much more troubling one in some respects. It is not simply that our identities are constituted by our memories—though, of course, they are, and this is crucially important—but also that the personhood of any of us, in its entirety, is created by and sustained within the loves and associations and affinities that shape us. There is no such thing as a person in separation. Personhood as such, in fact, is not a condition possible for an isolated substance. It is an act, not a thing, and it is achieved only in and through a history of relations with others. We are finite beings in a state of becoming, and in us there is nothing that is not action, dynamism, an emergence into a fuller (or a retreat into a more impoverished) existence. And so, as I said in my First Meditation, we *are* those others who make us. Spiritual personality is not mere individuality, nor is personal love one of its merely accidental conditions or extrinsic circumstances. A person is first and foremost a limitless capacity, a place where the all shows itself with a special inflection. We exist as "the place of the other," to borrow a phrase from Michel de Certeau. Surely this is the profoundest truth in the doctrine of resurrection. That we must rise from the dead to be saved is a claim not simply about resumed corporeality, whatever that might turn out to be, but more crucially about the fully restored existence of the person as socially, communally, corporately constituted. For Paul, flesh (σάρξ, *sarx*) and blood (αἷμα, *ʰaima*), the mortal life of the "psychical body" (σῶμα ψυχικόν, *sōma psychikon*), passes away, but not embodiment as such, not the "spiritual body" (σῶμα πνευματικόν, *sōma pnevmatikon*), which is surely not merely a local, but a communal condition: Each person is a body within the body of humanity, which exists in its proper nature only as the body of Christ.

   Where in this world, then, or in the world to come, does
the web of those associations that make us who we are reach
an end? Nowhere, I believe. Our personhood, to take the matter still further, must surely consist not only in the immediate
love of those close at hand, but also in our disposition toward
those whom we, by analogy, care for from afar, or even in the
abstract; for the most essential law of charity, of love when it
is truly active, is that it must inexorably grow beyond all immediately discernible boundaries in order to be fulfilled, and
to continue to be active. And all of those in whom each of
us is implicated, and who are implicated in each of us, are
themselves in turn implicated and intertwined in countless
others, on and on, without limit. We belong, of necessity, to
an indissoluble coinherence of souls. In the end, a person cannot begin or continue to be a person at all except in and by
way of all other persons. Gregory certainly understood this.
Human beings are not, in the metaphysical sense, "substantial relations" or pure acts of *perichoresis*—reciprocally "containing" one another—as the Persons of the Trinity are said to
be; we are not metaphysically simple in that way. According
to Sergei Bulgakov (1871–1944), in fact, only the Trinitarian
God is "personal" in the full sense, because in the simplicity
of his coinherent life of love he comprises every modality of
personal being: he is at once "I," "we," "thou," "you," but entirely as the one God. We are not that. And this means that we
require others in order to possess all the necessary and consti-
tutive modalities of true personal existence for ourselves. So, if
not subsistent relations, we are nonetheless, so long as we are
anything at all, subsistences of relationality; each of us is an
entire history of attachments and affinities, and none of those
attachments and affinities is merely accidental to some more
essential self. Yes, the psychological self within us—the small,

miserable empirical ego that so often struts and frets its hour upon the stage of this world—is a diminished, contracted, limited expression of spirit, one that must ultimately be reduced to nothing in each of us if we are to be free from what separates us from God and neighbor; but the unique personality upon which that ego is parasitic is not itself merely a chrysalis to be shed. There may be within each of us (indeed, there surely is) that divine light or spark of *nous* or spirit or *Atman* that is the abiding presence of God in us—the place of radical sustaining divine immanence, "nearer to me than my inmost parts," *interior intimo meo*—but that light is the one undifferentiated ground of our existence, not the particularity of our personal existences in and with one another. As spiritual persons, we are dynamic analogies of the simplicity of the divine life of love, and so belong eternally to that corporate identity that is, for Gregory of Nyssa, at once the "Human Being" of the first creation and also the eternal body of Christ.

But, then, this is to say that either all persons *must* be saved, or none *can* be. According to the traditional picture of a dual eternity, a final division of the saved and the damned (whether the latter be tortured forever or merely forever annihilated), God could in fact save no persons at all. He could of course erase each of the elect as whoever they once were, by shattering their memories and attachments like the gates of hell, and then raise up some other being in each of their places, thus converting the will of each into an idiot bliss stripped of the loves that made him or her *this* person—associations and attachments and pity and tenderness and all the rest. But persons, it seems, could not be saved; they could only be damned. Only in hell could any of us possess something like a personal destiny: tormented perhaps by the memories of the loves we squandered or betrayed, but not deprived of them altogether.

Is this, then, our choice after all: either a hell of eternal torment or a heaven that is the annihilation of everything that
ever made us who we were? If that is so, if to enter heaven we
must be reduced to anonymous essences, each indiscernibly
distinct from every other, perhaps it is to hell that we should
want to go. And that, as it happens, is where this part of my
argument ends. I began with the quotation from Pascal. Let me
draw to a close—a somewhat leisurely close—with one from
George MacDonald:

> Who, that loves his brother, would not, upheld by
> the love of Christ, and with a dim hope that in the
> far-off time there might be some help for him, arise
> from the company of the blessed, and walk down
> into the dismal regions of despair, to sit with the
> last, the only unredeemed, the Judas of his race,
> and be himself more blessed in the pains of hell,
> than in the glories of heaven? Who, in the midst
> of the golden harps and the white wings, knowing
> that one of his kind, one miserable brother in the
> old-world-time when men were taught to love their
> neighbour as themselves, was howling unheeded
> far below in the vaults of the creation, who, I say,
> would not feel that he must arise, that he had no
> choice, that, awful as it was, he must gird his loins,
> and go down into the smoke and the darkness and
> the fire, travelling the weary and fearful road into
> the far country to find his brother?—who, I mean,
> that had the mind of Christ, that had the love of
> the Father?
>
> (*Unspoken Sermons*, Series I:
> "Love Thy Neighbour")

This passage reminds me, as it happens, of certain of the teachings of Isaac of Nineveh, especially those regarding the nature of a truly merciful heart illuminated by God's love, which
is unable to contemplate even the sufferings of devils without tears of compassion. It reminds me as well of Silouan of
Athos's counsel to one of his brothers that true spiritual love
could never abide the sight of souls suffering in hell. It is quite
the opposite—the morally sane and spiritually enlightened
opposite, that is—of the degrading and barbaric nonsense that
the felicity of heaven could be increased by the saints' knowledge of the torments of the damned. MacDonald's words,
I think, indicate the only true sense in which the sufferings
of the damned could contribute to the beatitude of the saved:
by awakening again and yet again a truly substitutionary love
within souls whose whole being and delight consists precisely
in such love. And, really, if there is any true continuity between
the charity we are called to cultivate in this life and the transfiguring love that supposedly unites us to God, then surely
there can be no brake upon our desire to include those still
outside the company of the redeemed. Such love could find
its complete joy only in the joy of completion. Such love, in
fact, would not even be able to distinguish between this corporate desire for the salvation of all and the individual soul's
longing for its own salvation. I am not I in myself alone, but
only in all others. If, then, anyone is in hell, I too am partly in
hell. Happily, however, if the Christian story is true, that love
cannot now end in failure or tragedy. The descent into those
depths—where we seek out and find those who are lost, and
find our own salvation in so doing—is not a lonely act of spiritual heroism, or a futile rebellion of our finite wills against a
merciless eternity. For the whole substance of Christian faith
is the conviction that another has already and decisively gone

down into that abyss for us, to set all the prisoners free, even
from the chains of their own hatred and despair; and hence the
love that has made all of us who we are, and that will continue
throughout eternity to do so, cannot ultimately be rejected by
anyone. Thus all shall have their share in—as Gregory says in
his great mystical commentary *On the Song of Songs*—"the redeemed unity of all, united one with another by their conver-
gence upon the One Good." Only thus will humanity "according to the divine image" come into being, and only thus will
God be truly all in all.

Fourth Meditation

What Is Freedom?

A Reflection on the Rational Will

I

Let me begin again with a quotation, this one an anecdote recorded by Maurice Drury recounting an exchange between himself and Ludwig Wittgenstein:

> DRURY: I had been reading Origen before. Origen taught that at the end of time here would be a final restitution of all things. That even Satan and the fallen angels would be restored to their former glory. This was a conception that appealed to me — but it was at once condemned as heretical.

> WITTGENSTEIN: Of course it was rejected. It would make nonsense of everything else. If what we do now is to make no difference in the end, then all the seriousness of life is done away with. Your religious ideas have always seemed to me more Greek than biblical. Whereas my thoughts are one hundred per cent Hebraic.

> (Maurice O'Connor Drury, *Recollections of Wittgenstein*)

With all due respect to a revered philosopher, Wittgenstein's thinking in this matter was in fact no more Hebraic than it was Greek; indeed, it was no more Hebraic than it was Chinese, Aleut, Tasmanian, Argentine, or Venusian. He was speaking utter nonsense. But he was also, one has to note, a victim of the sort of conventional thinking about ancient Judaism, Graeco-Roman antiquity, and early Christianity that was dominant in his time and that, alas, probably remains dominant in ours. It is the sort of silly picture of the remote past that makes possible specious distinctions between the "Greek" and the "biblical" views of things, as if the religious and intellectual cultures of the ancient world were something like competing corporations or opposed systems of political ideology, hermetically sealed against one another. It is also, invariably, a picture that conforms more to our modern fantasies about the past than to the actual historical and textual evidence that scholars rely upon. In reality, the idea of eternal perdition for the wickedest of souls, in a place of unending suffering, appears to have been a Greek notion—mythological, religious, and philosophical—before it ever took (shallow) root in Jewish thought; it is certainly also an idea of only the most dubious "scriptural" authenticity. Plato's *Phaedo*, for example, contains a far more unambiguous theory of perpetual damnation than does any text found in the Bible. The spiritual vision common to the pagan world in which Christianity was born accommodated an immense range of speculations and beliefs and doubts regarding the nature and destiny of the human soul; but only a very few systems of religious thought were wholly free of terrifying opinions concerning what lay ahead for the reprobate or spiritually deluded. Platonism, the mystery cults of the time, Orphic sects, Neo-Pythagoreanism—apparently all of them could imagine some very dreadful fates indeed for those of us who fail to find the right path in this world, or the right path out of this world into the next. As for Wittgenstein's animadversions on Origen's views, they are nearly spectacular in their facile crudity. Certainly nothing in the genuine thought of Origen suggests that our conduct in this life does not matter; he certainly believed in and dreaded the torments of that refining and restoring fire that he believed awaits practically all of us. Frankly, anyone who thinks that what we do in this life can be "serious" only insofar as it figures into some sublimely fatuous game of chance, whose final stakes are absolutely all or nothing, suffers from a tragically diminutive moral imagination. It was precisely the absence of the banality of an eternal hell in Origen's thought that allowed him to believe that all of life and all of creation have a meaning, one immeasurably richer and more ravishing than some tawdry final division between the winners and losers of the game of history: the fullness of reality that will be achieved when all being is perfectly united to God, and God is all in all. For Origen 1 Corinthians 15 was the great key to the whole of the Christian mystery.

I suppose one ought not to judge Wittgenstein too harshly here, however. His error was no more egregious than are those of most professed Christians on these issues. Really, on the whole, Christians rarely pay particularly close attention to what the Bible actually says, for the simple reason that the texts defy synthesis in a canon of exact doctrines, and yet most Christians rely on doctrinal canons. Theologians are often the most cavalier in their treatment of the texts, chiefly because their first loyalty is usually to the grand systems of belief they have devised or adopted; but the Bible is not a system. A very great deal of theological tradition consists therefore in explaining away those aspects of scripture that contradict the finely wrought structure of this or that orthodoxy. To take a few obvious examples: The broad mainstream of Western Christian thought from the late fourth century on—albeit with many significant exceptions—has insisted that God's elect are eternally chosen not on the basis of God's foresight with regard to them, but solely as an act of sovereign power; and yet the only two verses in the New Testament that explicitly address the matter (Romans 8:29; 1 Peter 1:2) say precisely the opposite. Reformed tradition has long propounded the nauseating doctrine of "limited atonement" (and, if you are unacquainted with it, I will not rob you of your enviable innocence); and yet the sole scriptural pronouncement on the matter (1 John 2:2) rejects the notion out of hand. No principle is more deeply embedded in the soil of Protestant belief than the assertion that we are saved not by works but "by faith alone"; and yet the only appearance of this phrase in the whole of the New Testament (James 2:24) is in a verse that exactly contradicts such a claim. And how many modern Evangelicals think of salvation as something one receives by "accepting Jesus" as one's "personal lord and savior," even though such language is wholly absent from the New Testament, and even though all the real scriptural language of salvation is about a corporate condition of sacramental, moral, and spiritual union with the "body of Christ"? There are very venerable theological answers to all these apparent difficulties (well, except for the last one); but, of course, they are all disingenuous (in a quite unintentional way, no doubt), and consist mostly in ridiculous attempts to explain why the texts in question mean not what they say, but precisely what they deny. It has always been thus. That long inventory of seemingly universalist scriptural pericopes that I supplied in my Second Meditation has been explained away, in its every discrete item, again and again down the centuries of Christian history. Often the effect has been absurd. From the time of Augustine, for instance, it has been obligatory for devout infernalists to insist that in the space of a single verse (Romans 5:18)—of a single sentence, in fact—the word "all" changes from a reference to every human being throughout the whole of time into a reference solely to the limited number of those elected for salvation, and does so without the least notice being given. One should simply know that that is what Paul meant to say. This is preposterous, obviously, but settled orthodoxies so often are.

Perhaps, then, a little willful perversity might have a salutary effect here. What if one were to be so eccentric in one's hermeneutical method as to choose not to rationalize those universalist verses away, or not to treat them as hyperboles casually tossed off by authors too lethargic to be precise, and to elect instead to take them with the utmost seriousness, to recognize how numerous they are, and to attempt to understand the gospel in the light of the promises they seem to advance? This, at least, was the approach taken by Gregory of Nyssa. And, to be honest, I know of no interpreter of the New Testament whose readings of the text are more comprehensive, more coherent, or more rigorously faithful to the words on the page. Not that most modern Christians are likely to see this, at least not all at once. Most are captives of systems of theology that arose in the sixteenth century and after—this is true even of most Catholics—which were so remote in sensibility and conceptual structure from the world of the first century that they scarcely retained anything of the intellectual atmosphere and natural idiom of the Evangelists and Apostles, and which incorporated distinctly modern notions about such things as the nature of sovereignty and the logic of rational freedom. And then even those whose faith has not been entirely shaped by early modern thinking, in the churches of East and West, still tend to read the texts through centuries of later theological developments, many of which (to be perfectly honest) are more accidents of history than natural consequences of the tradition. I will not argue the specifics of that claim here. Rather, let me simply propose that we grant that Gregory—removed though he was by three centuries from the time of the Apostles—understood the original Greek terms of the Bible better than do most modern Christians, and that he inhabited an intellectual and religious world much nearer that of the New Testament than ours is, and then consider whether he might have known what he was talking about after all.

We should also ask why his theology was so *thoroughly* universalist. I can think of a number of answers that one might extract from his writings. The first is that he clearly believed universal salvation in Christ to be the true testimony of scripture, and the only theological position that could adequately account for every dimension of the New Testament's principal theological claims. Then, secondly, there was his understanding of the nature of humanity, as related to Christ and as bearing the image and likeness of God, and of the whole of humanity as enfolded within God's eternal intention of the Good (I discussed this in my previous meditation). Then, thirdly, there was his certainty that, in Christ, God's victory over evil and death was total, and that this triumph will be fully realized only when God is "all in all"—in the sense both that God will be "over all things" and that God will be "within all things" (including every rational will)—and when creation, by this perfect union with God, is finally fully raised up out of the nothingness from which God liberates it in making it exist. For him, therefore, the narrative of salvation in the New Testament was an epic tale of rescue and conquest, the overthrow of all evil—natural evil, moral evil, the evil of the hell we bring upon ourselves—and the invasion of death's kingdom by the shattering divinity of Christ. It is a tale that can end only in perfect victory and perfect peace. Then, fourthly, there was his belief that the punishments of the life to come are (as Paul suggests in 1 Corinthians 3) merely the final, purgative completion of this act of rescue and restoration, the harsh but necessary means for bringing about the ultimate purification of every soul—like the cautery or knife wielded by a surgeon, or like an implement for stripping clay from a rope. And then, finally, there was his metaphysical—but also biblical—conviction regarding the inherent finitude of evil, the infinite fullness of God's goodness, and the irrepressible dynamism of the moral life of rational spirits. He accepted, naturally, the definition of evil as a purely privative reality, with no substance or nature of its own, since God alone is the source of all being and "in him there is no darkness at all." He believed also that finite natures are necessarily dynamic realities, constituted as much by change as by formal stability, and that a finite rational being exists only in its act of moral and ontological desire for the Good, ever in motion. And he believed, of course, that God alone is the infinite plenitude of being and goodness that every soul seeks, by union with whom the soul is transformed into an eternally expanding vessel of divinity, an infinite capacity for love and knowledge transfigured forever—again, as Paul says—"from glory to glory" (2 Corinthians 3:18). For Gregory, therefore, no rational will could ever be fixed forever in the embrace of evil, since evil has nothing with which to hold on to that soul. In *On the Making of Humanity*, Gregory likened evil in creation to the shadow cast by the earth (which, according to the cosmology of the time, was how night was understood): a diminishing cone of darkness dying away weakly in a uni-

verse of light. Sooner or later, the rational will must exhaust
even its furthest reaches.

In my experience, as it happens, this last line of reasoning
is the one of Gregory's that seems the most exotic and logically
fragile to many modern readers. This is unfortunate, inasmuch
as the argument is in fact absolutely correct.

II

The most impressive and complete alternative to Gregory's
vision to come down to us from the golden age of the church
fathers would certainly be Augustine's, as I have already
noted. *The City of God* constitutes the most systematic, most
brilliantly constructed, most gracefully written account of
the gospel not as the glorious epic of rescue and restoration
that it was for Gregory and others of his ilk, but instead as a
strange and compelling tragicomedy, fraught with only partially dispelled shadows, consummated not in the perfect harmony of all beings (as envisaged by Gregory), but rather in
an ultimate division and unreconciled dissonance between a
realm of resplendent beauty and another of abysmal misery.
It is grand and grim and somehow gorgeous. And, as I have
made obvious to this point, and shall continue to make obvious below, I have any number of intellectual and critical reasons for rejecting the story that Augustine tells there, at least
in its closing phases—any number of philosophical complaints
to make against it, any number of objections to the scriptural
hermeneutics informing it, and so on—but, in the end, it is
my most spontaneously affective reason for rejecting it that
remains paramount for me: it is a tale that seems to me to reduce all of existence to a cruel absurdity. If the story really does
end as Augustine and countless others over the centuries have

claimed it must, with most—or, at any rate, very many . . . or, really, any—beings consigned to eternal torment, and if this story then also entails that God freely and needlessly created the world knowing that this would be the result, then Christianity has no "evangel"—no "good news"—to impart. There is only the hideous truth of a monstrous deity presiding over an evil world whose very existence is an act of cruelty, meaninglessly embellished with the additional narrative detail—almost parodic in its triviality—of the arbitrary salvation of a few select souls who are not even in any special sense deserving of the privilege (else grace were not grace, and absolute power were not absolute power). This is in fact the ghastliest possible "dysangel," the direst tidings ever visited on a world already too much burdened by unmerited suffering. To believe it even in part is to have all the reason one could ever need for refusing to procreate, and for regarding the world with a hatred that even the starkest "gnostic" dualism could not rival. And, truly to believe it in its own terms, one must at some level have lost the capacity to distinguish clearly between love and spite.

Then again, this has often been true of Christian thinking, going back quite a way. Once again, there is the glaring example of Thomas's defense of Peter Lombard's (genuinely sadistic) idea that the saints in heaven receive an increase in their beatitude from their knowledge of the tortures of the damned. But it would be disingenuous to displace the blame to so late a moment in Christian history. Perhaps, as I mentioned in my First Meditation, one sees this spitefulness well before Augustine's time in an earlier North African father, Tertullian, promising that one day Christians would not be persecuted, and indeed would be able instead to rejoice in the spectacle of the destruction of the wicked. Somehow, though, it is a more chilling thing when one sees it attenuated to the bloodless blandness of Thomas's formulation, in a form so demure and tepidly dispassionate as to make crystal clear just how thoroughly an indurated moral imbecility can come to seem like simple common sense, even for a brilliant thinker. And yet Thomas is still not to blame (not entirely, at least). He was the victim not only of a defective narrative, but also of the rigor of his own mind. Accepting, as he felt he had to do, the doctrine of hell's eternity, he was obliged to make sense of it somehow or other. He believed also, however, that the blessed soul's vision of God must be nothing less than a direct knowledge of Truth; it could not, therefore, involve any degree of ignorance of reality. So, of course, for him it was beyond question that the saints in heaven, rapt up in their ecstatic contemplation of the divine essence, must also know therein the fullness of creation in all its dimensions, including hell. He believed as well that all God's acts are for an end, and an end proper to God's own eternal goodness. And he was certain, of course, that the joys of the beatific vision must of their nature be perfect, and hence wholly unmarred by any shadow of sorrow or pity. Thus, in order to affirm that the sufferings of the damned—not only in themselves, but also as known to the saints—must conduce to some good, he could scarcely have arrived at any other conclusion than the one he reached. It was a horrid and contradictory conclusion, of course, but a sufficiently nimble theologian can generally get around that by the simple expedient of evacuating words like "justice" and "love" of any coherent content, and then reapplying them to the tale in their now newly pliant and aptly meaningless forms.

By any rational measure, after all, an eternal hell of torment would seem to lie wholly outside any order of the good that is—as the eternal vision of God supposedly must be—wholly sufficient in itself. Moreover, the idea of a punishment that does not serve an ameliorative purpose—as, by definition, eternal punishment cannot—should be a scandal to any sane conscience. Endless torture, never eventuating in the reform or moral improvement of the soul that endures it, is in itself an infinite banality. A lesson that requires an eternity to impart is a lesson that can never be learned. So, if one must make sense of the senseless here, then one must find some "greater good" in what to all appearances would be an unmitigated evil. So it was that the Lombard and Thomas arrived at their "amplifi-cation of beatitude" argument, since this endues hell with at least an extrinsic value. It was a poignantly desperate attempt to find some purpose in what would otherwise obviously be recognizable as an endless act of needless vindictiveness. But it is an absurd and depraved argument from every imaginable angle. To begin with, there is something inherently silly about the notion that God—the infinite wellspring of all Goodness, Truth, Beauty, and Being—would not be sufficient in himself to communicate the perfect knowledge of the Good and the happiness it entails to rational natures, formed for no other end than seeking union with him, when they are joined to him in eternity. It is nonsensical to think that the knowledge of his goodness could require or even allow for rational clarifi-cation—or that the soul's rational pleasure in that knowledge could be susceptible of increase—by way of some negative contrast, such as the sufferings of the damned. If a rational creature formed in the divine image required such a contrast fully to know God's goodness, then God's self-revelation as the Good in creatures could never be complete in itself. It would of its nature always require the "negative probation" of what is contrary to the Good. There would then, it seems, be some de-ficiency in the divine essence, some lack that would prevent it from supplying immediate and perfect satisfaction to a rational nature, some good end for rational intellects and wills that God in himself would be impotent to accomplish. The goodness of the divine essence, as known by a created spirit, would thus always be a relative value, and always parasitic upon the substantial difference between heaven and hell. Hell would then be part of God in an ultimate and therefore original sense: part of who he is *ad extra* but also, by virtue of this inherent dependency on evil for his self-revelation, part also of who he is *in seipso*. But this is absurd. As infinite Truth and Goodness, God must be the whole proper end of the rational will, and must therefore be able in himself to fulfill the rational appetite for truth and happiness. The soul needs nothing in addition to the divine nature in which it is called to partake (2 Peter 1:4), and certainly not the supplement of either a natural or a moral evil. And then too, of course, there is something even more degrading in the notion that creatures fashioned in the divine image might justly be reduced to an instrumental means to a didactic end—and this by way of unremitting suffering and despair. The only knowledge that could be won at that price would be the knowledge of an evil god.

Curiously enough, this last option too has often been taken by theologians and believers down the centuries—though not, of course, in quite such candid terms. I will not rehearse again the traditional arguments for the infernalist position from the tedious and grotesque principle of God's absolute sovereignty. Who cares that God is understood to be omnipotent? Everyone can grant that. The special Christian claim, however, is that this omnipotent God is also infinite love. There is something coarse and foolish about borrowing our picture of God (as did so many of the Reformers, Protestant and Catholic alike) from the early modern ideology of absolute monarchy and of total sovereignty. It results in a

way of thinking about God that is clearly antithetical to everything that the healthier Christian tradition says was revealed
about God in Christ, and that simply embraces moral imbecility under the form of an awesome "paradox." Admittedly,
it is a way of thinking adumbrated in theological tradition at
least as early as the late fourth century. Theologians are only
human, after all. But the keener consciences among believers
have always recognized that the Christian story of creation, redemption, and cosmic restoration is not a celebration of some
brute display of divine glory, whose ultimate meaning is nothing more than the banal tautology that God can do what God
does; rather, it is a claim about the revelation of God's nature
as a goodness that truly is infinite love, essentially and irreducibly. Hence, the only defense of the infernalist position that
is logically and morally worthy of being either taken seriously
or refuted scrupulously is the argument from free will: that
hell exists simply because, in order for a creature to be able to
love God freely, there must be some real alternative to God
open to that creature's power of choice, and that hell therefore
is a state the apostate soul has chosen for itself in perfect freedom, and that the permanency of hell is testament only to how
absolute that freedom is. This argument too is wrong in every
way, but not contemptibly so. Logically it cannot be true; but
morally it can be held without doing irreparable harm to one's
understanding of goodness or of God, and so without requiring the mind to make a secret compromise with evil (explicitly, at least).

III

I have already touched upon the nature of rational freedom,
more than once, but—at the risk of repeating a few points—

I am going to do so again. Given how very radically the standard late modern concept of freedom (we can call it the "libertarian" model) differs from that of most of ancient and
mediaeval intellectual culture, I want to make sure that the
matter has been made perfectly clear. So here I want to gather
up the half-statements I have left littering the path behind me
to this point, and try to integrate them into a somewhat more
continuous pattern of claims. One need not, incidentally, presume any aspect of Christian doctrine in order to grasp the
logical issues involved; but, if one does happen to presuppose
certain things intrinsic to the Christian view of reality, one has
already tacitly conceded enough to make the case I want to
advance. Above all, a Christian is more or less obliged to believe that there is such a thing as an intrinsic nature in rational spirits: We are created, that is to say, according to a divine
design, after the divine image, oriented toward a divine purpose, and thus are fulfilled in ourselves only insofar as we can
achieve the perfection of our natures in union with God. There
alone our true happiness lies. This inevitably places Christian
thought in the classical moral and metaphysical tradition that
assumes that true freedom consists in the realization of a complex nature in its own proper good (the "intellectualist" model
of freedom, as I have called it above). Freedom is a being's
power to flourish as what it naturally is, to become ever more
fully what it is. The freedom of an oak seed is its uninterrupted
growth into an oak tree. The freedom of a rational spirit is its
consummation in union with God. Freedom is never then the
mere "negative liberty" of indeterminate openness to everything; if rational liberty consisted in simple indeterminacy of
the will, then no fruitful distinction could be made between
personal agency and pure impersonal impulse or pure chance.
And this classical and Christian understanding of freedom re-

quires a belief not only in the reality of created natures, which must flourish to be free, but also in the transcendent Good toward which rational natures are necessarily oriented. To be fully free is to be joined to that end for which our natures were originally framed, and for which, in the deepest reaches of our souls, we ceaselessly yearn. Whatever separates us from that end, even if it be our own power of choice, is a form of bondage to the irrational. We are free not because we can choose, but only when we have chosen well. And to choose well we must ever more clearly see the "sun of the Good" (to employ the lovely Platonic metaphor), and to see more clearly we must continue to choose well; and the more we are emancipated from illusion and caprice, and the more our will is informed by and responds to the Good, the more perfect our vision becomes, and the less there is really to choose. Thus it is that Augustine could say that the consummation of freedom for a rational creature would be to achieve not the liberty attributed by tradition to Adam and Eve, who were merely "able not to sin" (*posse non peccare*), but rather the truest liberty of all, that of being entirely "unable to sin" (*non posse peccare*). To this state one can attain only when one's nature has been so emancipated from error that nothing can prevent it from reaching and enjoying the only end that can fulfill it: God. Only then is a rational being not a slave to ignorance and delusion.

At the same time, rationality must by definition be intentionality: the mind's awareness, that is, of a purpose it seeks or an end it wishes to achieve or a meaning it wishes to affirm. Rational freedom, in its every action, must be teleological in structure: one must know the end one is choosing, and why. Any act of the mind or will done without a reason, conversely, would be by definition irrational and therefore a symptom of bondage to something outside of or lower than the rational will. It is not even very sensible to ask, then, whether a free will might not "spontaneously" posit an end for itself out of the sheer exuberance of its power to choose, and then pursue that end out of pure unreasoning perversity. Absolute spontaneity would be an unfree act, a mere brute event beyond the control of mind and desire, while merely partial spontaneity would still be guided by some kind of purpose. If you wish to prove this to yourself, you need only attempt freely to posit an end for yourself without rationale. Then again, do not bother, since you would not actually be acting without rationale; you would instead be pursuing the conscious purpose of following my suggestion that you try to act spontaneously. Anything you might willfully choose to do for the *purpose* of doing something arbitrary would not, in fact, be arbitrary. And you will find also that even that supposedly arbitrary act, if you conceived of it before doing it, was not really arbitrary after all, but rather corresponded to some concrete intention that you knowingly chose, and for some specific reason, out of a strictly limited range of possible options. This too you can prove to yourself. You would not, for instance, simply in order to try to prove me wrong, leap off the top of a high building. Or, rather, if you did, the rest of us would immediately recognize your action as a feat of lunacy, and therefore not truly free. You cannot actually force yourself to behave "irrationally" except in an ultimately rational way. And to seek to find a first moment of perfect mindless impulse in any free act is to pursue a hopeless descent back along an infinite regress.

Hence, the traditional claim that the rational will can never choose evil as an end in itself, but only as a kind of terminal "good" in which to come to an only provisional rest: the Good *sub contrario,* as it were, but the Good even so. The whole of classical Christian tradition, after all, understands God himself as the source and end of all being, and hence as the Good as such. Thus the ontological status of evil must be a pure "privation of the good" (a view often mistakenly said to have been invented by Augustine, but in fact one long antedating him, in both pagan and Christian thought). Having no proper substance, evil cannot constitute the final cause or transcendental horizon of the natural will of any rational being; to suggest otherwise is to embrace an ultimate ontological, moral, and epistemological nihilism; it is to suggest that God himself is not the one Good of all beings, the one rational end of desire. Whatever one wishes must then be what one sees as being "good" in some sense or other, however perversely. Even Milton's Satan elects evil only as encompassed within this more original and more ultimate—this transcendental—longing:

> So farewell hope, and with hope farewell fear,
> Farewell remorse; all good to me is lost.
> Evil, be thou my good.
>
> (*Paradise Lost,* ll. 108–110)

It may be folly on Satan's part to attempt to choose the evil as his good, but it would be simple insanity for him to attempt to choose evil as truly evil *for him.* In itself, therefore, evil has no power to draw the rational will to itself, no substance to offer, no happiness to impart, no beauty with which to delight the soul. It cannot bring a rational nature to fulfilment, but can only thwart reason and desire. Therefore it can never form the original or ultimate purpose of the will. It cannot be the deepest motivation of any action at all. It can at most serve as a proximate end, veiling the truly ultimate end that prompts the will to pursue it.

Again, you can confirm this for yourself, quite apart from

any specific religious or metaphysical commitments. You need only examine your own motivations and deeds at any given moment of decision. The will, when freely moved, does nothing except toward an end: conceived, perceived, imagined, hoped for, resolved upon . . . Desire and knowledge, in a single impulse, direct any expression of free agency according to some purpose present to the mind, even if only vaguely. Otherwise, there is no act at all. And, if you consult your own experiences of personal agency, you will find that there are only two possible ways in which you can pursue any purpose that your mind might conceive: either as an end in itself or for the sake of an end beyond itself. But then, if you reflect a little longer on the matter, you will find that no finite object or purpose can wholly attract the rational will in the latter way. A finite good can summon desire in a limited degree, in the way, say, that one's longing for a new violin might prompt one to "want" to work the extra hours that will allow one to pay for it. But, even then, no finite thing, not even a violin—not even an authentic Guarneri—is desirable simply in itself. It may constitute the more compelling end that makes the less compelling end of working those extra hours "desirable," but in itself it can evoke desire only on account of some yet more primordial and more general disposition of the appetites and the will. One desires the violin, that is to say, out of a more constant and general desire for the pleasure one takes in music; but then that desire is itself provoked by an even more general desire for happiness as such; but one desires happiness because, in a very general sense indeed, one wants what is "good" for oneself rather than what is "bad"; and even this perhaps is so because, in a still more general sense, one knows rationally—even perhaps drily and purely abstractly—that the good is to be sought and the bad fled, and one wants to participate in the good-

ness of things. If not for some always more original orientation toward an always more final end, the will would never act
in regard to finite objects at all; immanent desires are always
in a sense deferred toward some more remote, more transcendent purpose. All concretely limited aspirations of the will are
sustained within formally limitless aspirations of the will. In
the end, it turns out, the only objects of desire that are not reducible to other, more general objects of desire, and that are
thus desirable entirely in and of themselves, are certain universal, unconditional, and exalted ideals or (as they are traditionally called) transcendentals: that is, the intrinsic perfections of
being in its fullness—according to certain conventional reck-
onings, being and unity, truth, goodness, and beauty—which
metaphysical tradition also says are convertible with one another, and ultimately with reality as such. One may not be, in
any given instant, immediately conscious that one's rational
appetites have been excited by these transcendental ends; but
they are the constant and pervasive preoccupation of the rational will in the deepest springs of its actions.

This is why, inevitably, true freedom is contingent upon
true knowledge and true sanity of mind. To the very degree
that either of these is deficient, freedom is absent. And with
freedom goes culpability. No mind that possesses so much as
a glimmer of a consciousness of reality is wholly lacking in
liberty; but, by the same token, no mind save one possessing
absolutely undiminished consciousness of reality is wholly
free. This is why we rightly distinguish between acts performed
compos mentis and acts performed *non compos mentis,* and
why we determine someone's mental competency or incom-
petency in large part from how clearly he or she understands
the difference between actions that serve his or her good and
actions that do not. We know that the willing of happiness is

intrinsically sane, and that willing what can only make one unhappy—if not for some greater good—is intrinsically the result of some disorder of the mind. Moreover, Christians are required to believe that the Good is not merely a matter of personal evaluation, but an objective verity: God himself, in fact, the very ground of reality, who is not simply one truth among others, but Truth as such. The mind conformed to him is the very definition of mental sanity: a purely rational act united to its only true occasion and end. So, for anyone to be free, there must be a real correspondence between his or her mind and the structure of reality, and a rational cognizance on his or her part of what constitutes either the fulfilment or the ruin of a human soul. Where this rational cognizance is absent in a soul, there can be only aimlessness in the will, the indeterminacy of the unmoored victim of circumstance, which is the worst imaginable slavery to the accidental and the mindless. If then there is such a thing as eternal perdition as the result of an eternal refusal of repentance, it must also be the result of an eternal ignorance, and therefore has nothing really to do with freedom at all. So, no: Not only is an eternal free rejection of God unlikely; it is a logically vacuous idea.

For those who worry that this all amounts to a kind of metaphysical determinism of the will, I may not be able to provide perfect comfort. Of course it is a kind of determinism, but only at the transcendental level, and only because rational volition must be determinate to be anything at all. Rational will is by nature the capacity for intentional action, and so must exist as a clear relation between (in Aristotelian terms) the "origin of motion" within it and the "end" that prompts that motion— between, that is, its efficient and final causes. Freedom is a relation to reality, which means liberty from delusion. This divine determinism toward the transcendent Good, then, is precisely what freedom is for a rational nature. Even God could not create a rational being not oriented toward the Good, any more than he could create a reality in which $2 + 2 = 5$. That is not to deny that, within the embrace of this relation between the will's origin and its end in the Good (what, again, Maximus the Confessor calls our "natural will"), there is considerable room for deliberative liberty with regard to differing finite options (what Maximus calls the "gnomic will"), and considerable room in which to stray from the ideal path. But, even so, if a rational creature—one whose mind is entirely unimpaired and who has the capacity truly to know the substance and the consequences of the choice confronting him or her—is allowed, without coercion from any force extrinsic to his or her nature, to make a choice between a union with God in bliss that will utterly fulfill his or her nature in its deepest yearnings and a separation from God that will result in endless suffering and the total absence of his or her nature's satisfaction, only one truly *free* choice is possible. A fool might thrust his hand into the flame; only a lunatic would not then immediately withdraw it. To say that the only sane and therefore free natural end of the will is the Good is no more problematic than to say that the only sane and therefore free natural end of the intellect is Truth. Rational spirit could no more will evil on the grounds that it is truly evil than the intellect could believe something on the grounds that it is certainly false. So, yes, there is an original and ultimate divine determinism of the creature's intellect and will, and for just this reason there is such a thing as true freedom in the created realm. As on the cross (John 12:32), so in the whole of being: God frees souls by dragging them to himself.

IV

I have to admit that, despite all I have just said, it is not primarily on any of these metaphysical or logical grounds that I find the free will defense of eternal torment an especially absurd one (though I do take them to be decisive), but rather as a matter of simple empirical observation. Nothing in our existence is so clear and obvious and undeniable that any of us can ever possess the lucidity of mind it would require to make the kind of choice that, supposedly, one can be damned eternally for making or for failing to make. Anyone who plays the game of life in life's house knows that the invisible figure hidden in impenetrable shadows on the far side of the baize table not only never shows his hand, but never lets us see the stakes of the wager, and in fact never tells us the rules. I am not denying that there is such a thing as revelation; but I do deny that very many of us can claim to have been accorded such a thing directly. We believe obscurely, hopefully, on the testimony of others. The real, unmistakable, ultimately irrefutable revelation of reality to all of us is one that as yet lies ahead, at that unimaginable moment when—and in that undiscoverable place where—we will no longer see all things as in a glass darkly, but will instead be granted a vision of reality "face to face" (1 Corinthians 13:12). If we lived like gods above the sphere of the fixed stars, and saw all things in their eternal aspects in the light of the "Good beyond beings," then perhaps it would be meaningful to speak of our capacity freely to affirm or freely to reject the God who made us in any absolute sense. As it is, we have never known such powers, and never could in this life. What little we can know may guide us, and what little we can do may earn us some small reward or penalty; but heaven and hell, according to the received views, are absolute destinies, and we have in this life no capacity for the absolute. To me, the question of whether a soul could freely and eternally reject God—whether a rational nature could in unhindered freedom of intellect and will elect endless misery rather than eternal bliss—is not even worth the trouble of asking. Quite apart from the logical issues involved, it is a question that has no meaning in the world we actually inhabit.

In another sense, moreover, the free will defense fails even properly to define the terms of the choice it claims a soul can make. It is hard to exaggerate how large a metaphysical solecism it is to think of God either as an option that can be chosen out from a larger field of options or as a discrete cause that acts upon the will as a kind of external force. And yet, with surprising frequency, apologists for the infernalist view— even some trained philosophers—treat him as both. In part this is attributable to a tendency among certain modern Anglophone Christian philosophers, formed in the analytic tradition, to abandon the metaphysics of classical theism that Christian intellectual tradition has unanimously presumed from its early centuries, in favor of a frankly mythological picture of God: God conceived, that is, not as Being itself—the source and end of all reality, in which all things live and move and have their being (Acts 17:28)—but merely as one more being alongside all the beings who are, grander and older and more powerful than all the rest, but still merely a thing or a discrete entity. Seen thus, God would then be, to use the scholastic terminology, someone whose essence is distinct from his existence, and therefore someone who exists exactly as we do, by dependence upon some deeper, more general, more encompassing, logically prior source of existence. That would mean that creation is something literally in addition to—and the whole realm of being something larger and more original than—God. This constitutes, to my mind, not only a sad impoverishment of the Christian picture of God, but in fact a logical disaster. God then is reduced to "a god," like Zeus or Odin. To me, this seems utterly preposterous at the most basic philosophical level (but I have discussed that at length in my book *The Experience of God*, and there is no need to rehearse all the issues here in any event).

Perhaps, however, the free will defense requires just such a mythical sort of God. Because, if God really is "God" in the classical acceptation of the word—the transcendent plenitude of all reality, as well as an infinite act of consciousness and love—then all these concerns about discrete personal agency and autonomy of the will must vanish as just so many category errors. Christian philosophers as sober and respected as the Catholic thinker Eleanore Stump and the Reformed thinker Alvin Plantinga have argued that it does not lie in God's power to assure that all will be saved, for the salvation of each person is contingent on his or her free choice, and God cannot compel a free act and yet preserve it in its freedom. In the words of Stump, from an article of 1986, "It is not within the power even of an omnipotent entity to *make* a person freely will anything." In one sense this is true, of course, but mostly because the very concept of an "omnipotent entity" is contradictory. Real omnipotence would require a power coterminous with the whole of being, from its innermost wellsprings and principles to its outermost consequences and effects; it would even require possession of the power belonging to the deepest source of all the acts of every rational will, without operating as a rival force in contest with those movements—the power, that is, of the one who is, as Augustine says, not merely *superior summo meo* (higher than my utmost), but *interior intimo meo* (more inward than my inmost). None of that would be possible for an "entity," a particular discrete contingent being among other beings, who exists in the manner of a finite thing. But God is not an "entity." Neither, for that reason, is he some sort of particular object that one could choose or reject in the same way that one might elect either to drink a glass of wine or to pour it out in the dust. He is, rather, the fullness of Being and the transcendental horizon of reality that animates every single stirring of reason and desire, the always more remote end present within every more immediate end. Insofar as we are able freely to will anything at all, therefore, it is precisely because he is *making* us to do so: as at once the source of all action and intentionality in rational natures and also the transcendental object of rational desire that elicits every act of mind and will toward any purposes whatsoever.

The suggestion, then, that God—properly understood—could not assure that a person freely will one thing rather than another is simply false. Inasmuch as he acts upon the mind and will both as their final cause and also as the deepest source of their movements, he is already intrinsic to the very structure of reason and desire within the soul. He is not merely some external agency who would have to exercise coercion or external compulsion of a creature's intentions to bring them to the end he decrees. If he were, then the entire Christian doctrine of providence—the vital teaching that God can so order all conditions, circumstances, and contingencies among created things as to bring about everything he wills for his creatures while still not in any way violating the autonomy of secondary causality—would be a logical contradiction. God, in his omnipotence and omniscience, is wholly capable of determining the result of all secondary causes, including free will, while not acting as yet another discrete cause among them. In one sense, naturally, this is merely a function of the coincidence in his nature of omniscience and omnipotence. Knowing not only

all the events that constitute each individual life, but also all of
an agent's inner motives and predispositions and desires — all
thoughts, impulses, hopes, preferences, yearnings, and aver-
sions — and so knowing what choice any given soul will make
when confronted with certain options and situated among certain circumambient forces, God can (if nothing else) so arrange the shape of reality that all beings, one way or another,
come at the last upon the right path by way of their own freedom, in this life or the next. In a very limited way, of course, we
can all at times do something similar. If I entice a child, whom
I know to be in complete possession of her rational faculties,
to eat a slice of cake when she is hungry by presenting her no
other options except a bowl of sand and a scorpion, I have not
made her choice of the cake any less free even in making it (as
far as I am able to do so) inevitable. Even if I offer her another
slice of cake as well, knowing that it is one she will like considerably less, I can still accomplish much the same thing. And
God, being infinitely resourceful and infinitely knowledgeable,
can weave the whole of time into a perfectly coherent continuity whose ultimate result is that all circumstances and forces
conduce to the union of every creature with himself, and can
do this precisely by confronting every rational nature with
possibilities he knows they will realize through their own free
volitions. It is true that he might accomplish this by imposing
limited conditions of choice upon every life; but the conditions
of choice are always limited anyway, and deliberative freedom
is always capable of only a finite set of possible determinations.

Neither, though, can God be merely one option among
others, for the very simple reason that he is not just another
object alongside the willing agent or alongside other objects
of desire, but is rather the sole ultimate content of all rational
longing. Being himself the source and end of the real, God can

never be for the will simply one plausible terminus of desire in competition with another; he could never confront the intellect simply as a relative and evaluative good, from which one might *reasonably* turn to some other. He remains forever the encompassing final object that motivates and makes actual every choice, the Good that makes the will free in the first place. Even an act of apostasy, then, traced back to its most primordial impulse, is motivated by the desire for God. Even the satanist can embrace evil only insofar as he thinks it will satisfy a desire for what is most agreeable to his own nature. He is in error in the choice he makes, and is culpable to the degree that he abets the error willingly; but it is also then the case that, to the degree he knows the Good in itself, he cannot but desire it rationally. However the "gnomic" faculty may wander, the "natural" will animating it seeks only one ultimate end. You can reject a glass of wine absolutely; you can even reject evil in its (insubstantial) totality without any remainder of intentionality. Neither of these things possesses more than a finite allure in itself. But you cannot reject God except defectively, by having failed to recognize him as the primordial object of all your deepest longings, the very source of their activity. We cannot choose between him and some other end in an absolute sense; we can choose only between better or worse approaches to his transcendence. As I have said, to reject God is still, however obscurely and uncomprehendingly, to seek God.

This means also that God could never be, for the rational will, merely some extrinsic causality intruding upon the will's autonomy, or some irresistible heteronomous power overwhelming the feebler powers of the creature. He is freedom as such, the fiery energy that liberates the flame from the wood. He is the very power of agency. He is the Good that makes the rational will exist. He is the eternal infinite source of all

knowledge and all truth, of all love and delight in the object
of love, who enlivens and acts within every created act. As an
infinite and transcendental end, God's goodness may be indeterminate as regards proximate ends, and that very indeterminacy may be what allows for deliberative determinations. There
may be conflicts and confusions, mistakes and perversities in
the great middle distance of life; as Duns Scotus says, we frequently must deliberate between which aspect of the Good to
pursue, whether to be guided in any moment by our *affectio
iustitiae* (our sense of what is just) or the *affectio commodi* (our
sense of what is suitable or convenient); but the encircling horizon never alters, and the Sun of the Good never sets. No soul
can relent in its deepest motives from the will's constant and
consuming preoccupation with God. If this were not so, and
if reason had no natural, ontological, and necessary relation
to God as the final rationale in all desire and agency, then God
would himself be something separate from the Good as such,
and from rationality as such, and could attract the rational will
merely in the manner of a predilection. But then he would not
actually be God in any meaningful sense. In truth, he gives his
creatures freedom always by *making* them freely seek him as
the ultimate end in all else that intentional consciousness seeks.

Hence, again, should God providentially arrange the
contingencies of every life, and do so unremittingly till all evil
has vanished altogether—in this world and the world to come,
even if needs be by way of purgation—guiding every soul to
the only final end it can ever truly freely desire, this would be
no trespass upon the sanctity of the autonomous will. It would
be, rather, the act of bringing about the soul's only possible
true liberation, the full flowering of true freedom in a nature
that, till that point, has only ever partly known what it is to be
at liberty. Only the Truth can make you free (John 8:32). And

this, of course, all Christian traditions have always acknowledged, tacitly or explicitly. For the most part, however, these
traditions have started from the assumption that God's providence—for reasons best known only to him—avails for the
salvation of only a certain number of souls, while leaving the
rest to be lost, even though it clearly lies in his power to save
all by the same means if he should so wish. There is a very old
distinction in Christian teaching, going back at least as far as
John of Damascus (c. 675–749), between God's antecedent and
consequent decrees: between, that is, his original will for a creation unmarred by sin ("Plan A," so to speak) and his will for
creation in light of the fall of humanity ("Plan B"). And it has
usually been assumed that, whereas the former would have
encompassed all of creation in a single good end, the latter
merely provides for the rescue of only a tragically or arbitrarily
select portion of the race. But why? Perhaps the only difference, really, between these antecedent and consequent divine
decrees (assuming that such a distinction is worth making at
all) is the manner by which God accomplishes the one thing
he intends for creation from everlasting. Theologians and cate-
chists may have concluded that God would ideally have willed
only one purpose but must in practical terms now will two; but
logic gives us no reason to think so. Neither does scripture (at
least, not when correctly read). After all, "our savior God," as
1 Timothy 2:4 says, "intends *all* human beings to be saved and
to come to a full knowledge of truth."

V

And then, perhaps, there is an even more compelling reason
for rejecting the free will defense of hell: the person of Jesus
of Nazareth. Really, this should also be obvious. At least, it

must be the case that Christians are obliged to regard Jesus as having been a truly free creature during his life among human beings. Whatever powers he may have possessed by virtue of his divine nature, insofar as he was wholly human he must have lacked nothing intrinsic to whatever it is that makes human beings rational agents. I mention this only because one does occasionally hear it argued that the liberty to reject God absolutely, and to turn with finality toward evil, is a necessary and precious element of human nature, apart from which one would not be a true moral agent. Now, as I have just made clear, I regard the entire account of human freedom on which such a claim is based as logically incoherent and metaphysically confused. But, considered theologically, the claim may very well be an even more egregious contradiction of the whole tradition of orthodox Christology; it may, in fact, entail heresy. This certainly should pose something of a problem for anyone who professes belief in the teachings that define the faith. Maximus the Confessor, among the subtlest and most rigorous thinkers on the doctrine of Christ in the history of either Eastern or Western Christianity, was quite insistent that our "gnomic" will—our faculty of deliberation—is so wholly dependent upon our "natural" will—the innate and inextinguishable movement of rational volition toward God—that the former has no *actual* existence in us except when the defect of sin is present in our intellects and intentions. As such, the gnomic will may in fact be dependent upon the natural, but the absence of a gnomic will is in no sense a deficiency of our nature. More to the point, not only is the actuality of a *distinct* deliberative will an unnecessary dimension of our natures; so in fact is the very capacity for such a will. If this seems an extravagant supposition, it is no more than the conclusion that must be drawn from the entire logic of the Incarnation.

Could Christ have freely rejected the will of the Father, or rejected the divine Good as the proper end of his rational intentionality? Not only could he not have done so as a matter of actual fact; for just that reason, neither could he have possessed the capacity to do so. In truth, even the word "capacity" is misleading here, since such a susceptibility to sin would be a defect of the will rather than a natural power. The very thought that Christ might have turned from God, even as an abstract potential of his human nature, would make a nonsense of both Trinitarian and Christological doctrines. In the case of the former, it would contradict the claim that Christ is God of God, the divine Logos, the eternal Son whose whole being is the perfect expression of the Father, of one essence with Father and Spirit, rather than some mere creature outside the single intellect and will of God. In the latter, it would undermine the logic of the so-called enhypostatic union: the doctrine, that is, that there is but one person in Jesus, that he is not an amalgamation of two distinct centers of consciousness in extrinsic association, and that this one person, who possesses at once a wholly divine and a wholly human nature, is none other than the hypostasis, the divine Person, of the eternal Son. It is, after all, a cardinal principle of orthodox Christology that the integrity of Christ's humanity entails that he possesses a full and intact human will, and that this will is in no wise diminished or impaired by being "operated," so to speak, by a divine hypostasis whose will is simply God's own willing. So, if human nature required the real capacity freely to reject God, then Christ could not have been fully human. According to Maximus, however, Christ possesses no gnomic will at all, and this because his will was perfectly free.

Nor, incidentally, does it make any difference here to argue (as some, I feel sure, would want to do if pressed on this point) that the sinlessness of Jesus of Nazareth was no more than a special accident of the specific person he was, and that in every other sense his humanity would have been capable of sin had it been instantiated in some other person. This is meaningless. Deliberative liberty is nothing but the power of any given person to choose one end or another. The point remains, then, that a human being cannot be said to have the "capacity" for sin if sin is literally impossible for the person he is; and so, even if this capacity was wanting in just the single person that Jesus happened to be, while yet that single person truly possessed a full and undiminished human will and human mind, then the capacity to sin is no necessary or natural part of either human freedom or human nature. Rather, it must be at most a privation of the properly human, one whose ultimate disappearance would—far from hindering the human will—free human nature from a malignant and alien condition. What distinguished Christ in this regard from the rest of humanity, if Christological orthodoxy is to be believed, is not that he lacked a kind of freedom that all others possess, but that he was not subject to the kinds of extrinsic constraints upon his freedom (ignorance, delusion, corruption of the will, and so forth) that enslave the rest of the race. In Augustine's terms, he was—as we should all wish to become—incapable of (or, rather, not incapacitated by) any deviation from the Good. He had a perfect knowledge of the Good and was perfectly rational; hence, as a man he could not sin; hence, he alone among men was fully free.

So it is that we discover at the last, as could scarcely have been otherwise, that Gregory of Nyssa was right, and his reasoning unassailable. For him, all finite existence is change, and all finite rational will is an intentional movement toward an end. Evil, being nothing in itself, can never be an ultimate end, but must always subsist only as a privation of what is real. The irrepressible dynamism of human nature is, according to Gregory, simply what rational spirit is; if that nature were to cease freely to intend and seek an end, it would in that instant cease to exist altogether as conscious mind or vital desire. An intellectual and intentional act, being nothing but a movement toward an end, exists only as movement. Even the blessed soul's union with God, Gregory insisted, must consist for the creature in an eternal *epektasis,* an endless intentional and dynamic "stretching out" into an ever deeper participation in the divine nature. For any finite thing possessed of a principle of life—*psychē,* soul—movement is life, stasis death. Even in hell, a soul would exist as a soul only by freely intending what it wants. The restlessness of the rational will and intellect is directly convertible with the very existence of the rational creature. One can become distracted, I imagine, by the rather vivid imagery that Gregory uses, of a soul wandering in evil like a celestial body moving through the earth's shadow, until it necessarily reaches the shadow's limit; but he has a penetrating point to make. Given the dynamism of human nature, given its primordial longing for the Good, given the inherent emptiness of evil, given the finitude of evil's satisfactions and configurations and resources, no rational nature could freely persist forever in its apostasy from the Good. There is no power in that nature or in evil equal to such an act. As for whether God might somehow impose upon such a soul a perpetual delusion, so that the mind and will continue to move forever in the shadows, Gregory never considered it at all: in part, I expect, because he believed that the natural movement of the soul toward an end must be a truly free act in order to be real, and hence must always be concerned ultimately with the Good; and in part because he did not regard God as a sadistic monster.

Those who argue for the infernalist position from the principle of the soul's power to reject God freely have already begun their reasoning from a point located somewhere along the course of a logical circle. They recognize, correctly, that this act of rejection can be a perpetual state freely assumed by a soul only if that soul is free in perpetuity. A fixed state based on a decision made in the ever remoter past (billions and trillions and whole aeons of years in the past), in a state that logically could never have allowed for an entirely clear cognizance of reality, obviously could never truly be a freely assumed condition. The self-condemnation of the damned must be an eternally sustained rational action, not simply a *fait accompli* no longer subject to deliberative revision. But then they fail to recognize that this is a ridiculous picture of reality. For an act to be fully free, it must be undertaken *compos mentis,* uncompromised even by personal emotional or intellectual states that could obscure the soul's knowledge of what it is choosing and why. And so this notion — that a soul fully aware of who God is, and of how he alone could fulfill and beatify a rational nature, and suffering all the most extreme torments consequent upon turning from God and subjecting itself to an unnatural severance from the Good, could freely elect forever, successively, and continuously to dwell in misery — makes a mockery of the most basic logic of the very idea of created freedom. Now, of course, the infernalist can devise all sorts of clever evasions here, such as, say, trying to redefine temporal succession or intention or rational action in ways that seem to preserve the essence of each of these things, but that covertly destroy it. If, however, one undertakes to address the matter reasonably and honestly, one has to acknowledge that any truly free condition could be nothing other than the love of God. As Gregory understood, evil has no power to hold us, and we have no power to cling to evil; shadows cannot bind us, and we in turn cannot lay hold on them. In the end, God must be all in all.

I should note here as well, before finally drawing these meditations to a close, that for Gregory it would make no sense to suggest that God—who is by nature not only the source of Being, but also the Good and the True and the Beautiful and everything else that makes spirits exist as rational beings—would truly be all in all if the consummation of all things were to eventuate merely in a kind of extrinsic divine supremacy over creation. A mere god's reign over a world might consist in simple sovereignty over all things, and might be deemed complete if that god's "enemies" were merely objectively confined in some state of penal suffering. It is a horrific picture of things, but not incoherent. But God is not a god, and his final victory, as described in scripture, will consist not merely in his assumption of perfect supremacy "over all," but also in his ultimately being "all in all." Could there then be a final state of things in which God is all in all while yet there existed rational creatures whose inward worlds consisted in an eternal rejection of and rebellion against God as the sole and consuming and fulfilling end of the rational will's most essential nature? If this fictive and perverse interiority were to persist into eternity, would God's victory over every sphere of being really be complete? Or would that small, miserable, residual flicker of Promethean defiance remain forever as the one space in creation from which God has been successfully expelled? Surely it would. So it too must pass away. For one thing, that interior world is no small thing, really. For creatures, what appears to the rational will is reality as such, the whole of truth. The world exists for creatures as what is revealed to them in the very act of rational intentionality, of dynamic cognizance; intentional mind is not some narrow, vacant annex of reality, but is rather the place where the world shows itself, and so where it exists as *that* creature's world. Any rational will that does not surrender to God as the true end of desire and knowledge is a whole world from which God is absent, and so is God's defeat.

One cannot conjure this problem away, incidentally, simply by giving up on the notion of hell as eternal torment and adopting in its place the notion of a final annihilation for the damned (which, as I have already noted, has at least the virtue of conforming somewhat better to the large majority of the metaphors for eschatological condemnation found in scripture). The ultimate annihilation of all the wicked souls that have ever been would still not constitute the total victory promised in the fifteenth chapter of 1 Corinthians. It would perhaps demonstrate that God reigns "over all," at least by the end of the story, and in that sense it might suggest that God, for all intents and purposes, is "all" that is. But it would never allow for the reality of God being "all *in* all." *Sub specie aeternitatis*—and God is eternal and transcendent of time, after all—there would always be a fixed number of finite histories that ended in a divine absence, and so of inner rational wills where God was present only ever in a relative and partly negative degree. There would exist eternally the residual reality of souls that never surrendered to him, and within which consequently he never appeared as the sole and consuming end of knowledge and desire, recognized by the intellect and affirmed by the rational will—souls *in* which he was never the *all*. And then also, to return to the theme of my First Meditation, from this same eternal divine perspective these thwarted and ultimately annihilated rational natures would still constitute that irreducible tragic historical surd, that sacrifice that God was willing to throw away to secure the limited, relative, necessarily contingent goodness of his creative acts. This is not enough. This would be, frankly, an almost farcically drab, depressingly ambiguous anticlimax. Sergei Bulgakov, the most remarkable Christian theological mind of the twentieth century, was perhaps the nearest modern Orthodox thinker in sensibility to Gregory of Nyssa (and, really, to all the greatest of the early church fathers). For him, as a modern man, the imagery of inward landscapes—the territories of the soul—seemed more natural than the cosmological metaphors—heavenly bodies moving through the earth's ecliptic shadow—preferred by Gregory. His way of making Gregory's point, therefore, was to argue that heaven and hell exist within every rational nature, and that they do so in every case in a unique but dynamically altering balance. Freedom consists in the soul's journey through this interior world of constantly shifting conditions and perspectives, toward the only home that can ultimately liberate the wanderer from the exile of sin and illusion. And God, as the transcendent end that draws every rational will into actuality, never ceases setting every soul free, ever and again, until it finds that home. To the inevitable God, every soul is bound by its freedom. In the end, if God is God and spirit is spirit, and if there really is an inextinguishable rational freedom in every soul, evil itself must disappear in every intellect and will, and hell must be no more. Only then will God, both as the end of history and as that eternal source and end of beings who transcends history, be all in all. For God, as scripture says, is a consuming fire, and he must finally consume everything.

III

What May Be Believed

If others go to hell, then I will too. But I do not believe that; on the contrary I believe that all will be saved, myself with them—something which arouses my deepest amazement.

—SØREN KIERKEGAARD,
AUTOBIOGRAPHICAL JOURNALS

Final Remarks

Custom dictates and prudence advises that here, in closing, I wax gracefully disingenuous and declare that I am uncertain in my conclusions, that I offer them only hesitantly, that I entirely understand the views of those that take the opposite side of the argument, and that I fully respect contrary opinions on these matters. I find, however, whether on account of principle or of pride, that I am simply unable to do this. I believe I am obeying my conscience in refusing to lie about my convictions; more to the point, though, I believe that I am obeying my conscience with a special rigor in rejecting the majority view that there is a hell of eternal torment, since I am fairly sure that it must be a wicked thing to give one's intellectual assent to something one cannot help but find morally repugnant. I do not rely on conscience alone, however. Without the support of reason, all the conscientiousness in the world would still add up to nothing more than mere personal sentiment. I make no apologies whatsoever for entirely rejecting the late Augustinian tradition regarding the relation between grace and nature, predestination and inherited guilt, and most especially the early modern variants of that tradition (Calvinism, Baroque Thomism, Jansenism, and so forth) that brought it to such extreme expressions.

All of that way of seeing things, as a matter of simple historical fact, rests on catastrophic misreadings of scripture, abetted by bad translations and anachronistic assumptions regarding the conceptual vocabularies of the authors of the New Testament, as well as (in certain cases) very defective metaphysical reasoning. Even if this were not the case, however, that tradition's sheer moral wretchedness as a vision of the gospel would still render it unworthy of respect. All that said, however, I know also that in these pages I have gone far beyond a mere demurral with one particular stream of Christian thought. I have rejected every version of the infernalist orthodoxy, no matter which Christian tradition may have produced it, and no matter how tenderhearted the reasoning that informs it. To have done otherwise would have been dishonest on my part.

There was a time, in the early centuries of the church, and especially in the Eastern half of the imperial world, when it was still generally assumed that there were mysteries of the faith that should be reserved for only the very few, the Christian intellectual elite or *pnevmatikoi,* "spiritual persons" (a term used even by Paul), while the faith of the more common variety of believers should be nourished only with simpler, coarser, more infantile versions of doctrine. For the less learned, less refined, less philosophical Christians, it was widely believed, the prospect of hellfire was always the best possible means of promoting good behavior. Even among those who believed in an eventual salvation of all souls, there was perhaps an overly pronounced willingness to indulge in a hint of holy duplicity, if that was what it took to inspire spiritual sobriety in the more obdurately cruel and brutish of the baptized. Occasionally we catch a fugitive glimpse of this patronizing amphiboly in the texts that have come down to us, such as when the great Cappadocian father Gregory of Nazianzus (c. 329–390), in the course of a sermon on hellfire, pauses ever so slightly to wink mischievously, as it were, at his fellow sophisticates by mentioning that there are some who "take a more merciful view of this fire, in a way worthier of the one who punishes," and then promptly resumes his dire hellfire-and-brimstone admonitions to all those lesser intellects in the room (Oration 40.36). It may offend against our egalitarian principles today, but it was commonly assumed among the very educated of those times that the better part of humanity was something of a hapless rabble who could be made to behave responsibly only by the most terrifying coercions of their imaginations. Belief in universal salvation may have been far more widespread in the first four or five centuries of Christian history than it was in all the centuries that followed; but it was never, as a rule, encouraged in any general way by those in authority in the church.

Perhaps there was some wisdom in this. I am a late modern man, and cannot conquer my sense that one has to give everyone the same information if one is to be fair (and I want us all to be fair with one another). But this may be foolish of me. Maybe there are a great many among us who can be convinced to be good only through the threat of endless torture at the hands of an indefatigably vindictive God. Even so much as hint that the "purifying flames" of the Age to come will at the last be extinguished, and perhaps a good number of us will begin to think like the mafioso who refuses to turn state's evidence because he is sure that he can "do the time." Bravado is, after all, the chief virtue of the incorrigibly stupid. I hope that this is not really the case, but maybe I am being somewhat quixotic; my actual experiences provide me with at best ambiguous evidence in the matter. Still, I am not sufficiently phlegmatic to pull off the charade. I cannot prevaricate about something that strikes me as so very clear in its moral significance. And I certainly cannot believe what I find intrinsically unbelievable. I have never had much respect for the notion of the blind leap of faith, even when that leap is made in the direction of something beautiful and ennobling. I certainly cannot respect it when it is made in the direction of something intrinsically loathsome and degrading. And I believe that this is precisely what the infernalist position, no matter what form it takes, necessarily involves. I have tried to make an honest effort to find an exception to this rule. Over the years, I have dutifully explored all the arguments for hell's eternity from Christian antiquity to the present, philosophical and theological, and I continue to find them all manifestly absurd. Even the gentlest, the most morally delicate, the most judiciously reluctant all start, I believe, on the far side of a prior existential decision to accept an obviously ludicrous premise, and then to proceed as if that premise were not only doctrinally mandatory, but rationally inoffensive. God forbid, then, that we ever return to, or even so much as allow ourselves to recall, that initial moment, before rationalization began, and before that leap of faith was made.

In my introduction to this volume, I noted that I found it a strange experience to be writing a book that I expect will convince nearly no one. The truth is that I find it even more unsettling to have written a book that I believe ought never to have needed to be written in the first place. I honestly, perhaps guilelessly believe that the doctrine of eternal hell is *prima facie* nonsensical, for the simple reason that it cannot even be stated in Christian theological terms without a descent into equivocity so precipitous and total that nothing but edifying gibberish remains. To say that, on the one hand, God is infinitely good, perfectly just, and inexhaustibly loving, and that, on the other, he has created a world under such terms as oblige him either to impose, or to permit the imposition of, eternal misery on finite rational beings, is simply to embrace a complete contradiction. And, no matter how ingenious the rhetorical tricks one devises to convince oneself that the claim is in fact logically coherent, morally elevating, and spiritually enlivening, the contradiction remains unresolved. All becomes mystery, but only in the sense that it requires a very mysterious ability to believe impossible things. We all know this to be so, even if we refuse to know that we know it. To suggest, as it has occasionally been suggested to me, that I am rashly assuming that there is some ultimately irreconcilable incompatibility between the two sides of the infernalist orthodoxy is akin, in my mind, to suggesting that it is no more than arbitrary prejudice to assume that something cannot be at once A and not-A. At that point, I have no hope of convincing my disputants of anything. When the very principles of moral logic are called into doubt, at the level of their atomic "simples"—the very meanings, that is, of the discrete terms of moral reasoning—then one can, I imagine, have faith in anything, be it ever so atrocious. But again, as I say, I do not think this should need to be argued at all. If "justice" means anything at all, it cannot be that. If "love" means anything at all, it cannot be that. If "goodness" means anything at all, it cannot be that.

One need only consider what ludicrous strains we must place upon our imaginations and our reasoning to accept the very concept of a hell of eternal duration—for it must be a duration of which we are speaking, not some timeless eternity of the sort possible only for the infinite God. When we try to think in terms of an eternally successive state of conscious torment in any soul, are we able even to conceive what sort of rational content the idea might contain? Can we imagine—logically, I mean, not merely intuitively—that someone still in torment after a trillion ages, or then a trillion trillion, or then a trillion vigintillion, is in any meaningful sense the same agent who contracted some measurable quantity of personal guilt in that tiny, ever more vanishingly insubstantial gleam of an instant that constituted his or her terrestrial life? And can we do this even while realizing that, at that point, his or her sufferings have in a sense only just begun, and in fact will always have only just begun? What extraordinary violence we must do both to our reason and to our moral intelligence (not to mention simple good taste) to make this horrid notion seem palatable to ourselves, and all because we have somehow, foolishly, allowed ourselves to be convinced that this is what we *must* believe. Really, could we truly believe it at all apart from either profound personal fear or profound personal cruelty? Which is why, again, I do not believe that most Christians truly believe what they believe they believe. After the public dissemination of my first lecture on these matters in 2015, one of the more truculent assaults on my arguments came from an ordained convert to Eastern Orthodoxy who several times chided me online for failing to grasp that eternal damnation is proper for finite transgressions because (as he tirelessly, oracularly repeated) *"time is the foundation of eternity."* He was quite unconscious that, far from offering a solution to the apparent moral scandal in the traditional theology of hell, he was simply reiterating it. After all, it would be a very curious architect indeed who would think an infinite edifice erected upon an ever more infinitesimal foundation a well-conceived and duly proportioned design, even if he had the power to bring it about. And, if we cannot properly imagine that and really believe in it, we certainly cannot properly imagine an eternity of misery erected upon a temporal span that is, by comparison, scarcely more than nothing, and then actually convince ourselves that such a thing is morally possible. We can think that we believe it all, but only so long as we do not pause too long to consider what we are doing.

It was not always thus. Let me, at least, shamelessly idealize the distant past for a moment. In its dawn, the gospel was a proclamation principally of a divine victory that had been won over death and sin, and over the spiritual powers of rebellion against God that dwell on high, and here below, and under the earth. It announced itself truly as the "good tidings" of a campaign of divine rescue on the part of a loving God, who by the sending of his Son into the world, and even into the kingdom of death, had liberated his creatures from slavery to a false and merciless master, and had opened a way into the Kingdom of Heaven, in which all of creation would be glorified by the direct presence of God. It was an announcement that came wrapped in all the religious and prophetic and eschatological imagery of its time and place, and armored in the whole metaphorical panoply of late antique religion, but with far less of the background and far fewer of the details filled in than later Christians would have found tolerable. It was, above all, a joyous proclamation, and a call to a lost people to find their true home at last, in their Father's house. It did not initially make its appeal to human hearts by forcing them to revert to some childish or bestial cruelty latent in their natures; rather, it sought to awaken them to a new form of life, one whose premise was charity. Nor was it a religion offering only a psychological salve for individual anxieties regarding personal salvation. It was a summons to a new and corporate way of life, salvation by entry into a community of love. Hope in heaven and fear of hell were ever present, but also sublimely inchoate, and susceptible of elaboration in any number of conceptual shapes. Nothing as yet was fixed except the certainty that Jesus was now Lord over all things, and would ultimately yield all things up to the Father so that God might be all in all.

I would not say, however, that the gradual hardening of the church's teachings on hell into the infernalist orthodoxy, over half a millennium, was merely an accident of history. It may have been much more a necessity of culture, or of politics, or even of psychology. At least, if I allow myself to take the cynical view of the matter, I cannot help but believe that the infernalist view was fated to prevail simply as an institutional imperative (or, at any rate, an institutional convenience). The more the church took shape as an administrative hierarchy, and especially as it became an organ of and support for imperial unity and power, the more naturally it tended to command submission from the faithful by whatever permissible methods of persuasion lay near at hand. I do not mean that some nefarious conspiracy of bishops and priests consciously and deviously set about elevating the infernalist view over alternative theories as a means of subduing a stupid and fractious laity. I mean merely that institutions all but inevitably evolve into those configurations—structural, ideological, ethical, emotional—that best fortify their power, influence, and stability. And fear is a majestically potent instrument. If I were to take an even more expansively cynical view of the matter, I would add that the work of "civilizing" barbaric populations has always been advanced in part—especially among those persons or peoples whom the patrician classes regard as temperamentally recalcitrant or intellectually feeble—by searing consciences into intractable natures through the regular application of the cautery of terror. By those same means, moreover, institutions can also render restive and inquisitive minds docile. Terror, one might argue, works its magic equally well in natures brutishly indomitable and irrepressibly curious.

On the other hand, to take a somewhat less jaded view of the matter, one should not underestimate the need to offer believers a complete picture of things, which no great religious movement can afford to ignore. Born as it was in late antiquity, the church inherited, and for many centuries preserved, the grand cosmic architecture of the Ptolemaic physical universe; what it further required, however, and what the religious environment of late antiquity could only partially supply, was a complementary spiritual architecture, a mythic hierarchy to fill out and complete the cosmic, one with fixed dimensions and levels and latitudes. And the picture that ultimately developed, reaching from God's empyrean above all the way down to the absolute abyss of hell below, encompassed a complete cosmic and spiritual ecology, filled with tenebrous depths and radiant heights, mysteries and terrors, delights and struggles and defeats and triumphs. One need only read Dante to see how all of this could flower into a fully realized and gloriously rich—if also perhaps dispiritingly grim—vision of reality, one in which there was boundless room for the mind and imagination to wander and grow and create. Every civilization requires a mythic frame. But, that said, that picture of the universe has for the most part passed away already. Certainly all its physical features have disappeared from our vision of reality. Perhaps it is past time that we considered whether the spiritual structure of that vanished cosmos, at least in some of its more garish details, could disappear as well without any great damage to our religious imaginations. We might, in fact, find the picture considerably improved.

I could go on. I could, if nothing else, spend a few hundred pages more dealing with certain highly technical issues of Christian metaphysical tradition (and, for reasons or preoccupations of my own, with what I take to be a host of problems with certain forms of "manualist" Thomism, which I see as being wrong on all these matters in only the most interesting ways). But I do not think that it would actually add anything to the essential arguments of these pages. As I stated at the beginning of this book, the two exceedingly simple—almost childish—questions that have persistently bothered me down the years, whenever I have tried to make sense of the doctrine of a hell of eternal torment, are whether it lies within the power of any finite rational creature freely to reject God, and to do so with eternal finality, and whether a God who could create a world in which the eternal perdition of rational spirits is even a possibility could be not only good, but the transcendent Good as such. And, for the reasons I have given above, I believe that the answer to both questions must be an unqualified and un-yielding no.

I have been asked more than once in the last few years whether, if I were to become convinced that Christian adher-ence absolutely requires a belief in a hell of eternal torment, this would constitute in my mind proof that Christianity should be dismissed as a self-evidently morally obtuse and logically incoherent faith. And, as it happens, it would. As I say, for me it is a matter of conscience, which is after all only a name for the natural will's aboriginal and constant orienta-tion toward the Good when that orientation expresses itself in our conscious motives. As such, conscience must not abide by the rule of the majority. Placed in the balance over against its dictates, the authority of a dominant tradition or of a reigning opinion has no weight whatever. And my conscience forbids assent to a picture of reality that I regard as morally corrupt, contrary to justice, perverse, inexcusably cruel, deeply irratio-nal, and essentially wicked. Nor do I believe that this is arro-gance on my part. For me, the option of such assent simply does not lie open. It is not even conceivable. Whether in the midst of our wisdom or of our folly, of truth or of error, it is the transcendental horizon of all things that continually calls us to itself, and we must obey as best we can. We may revere tradition or respect the sincerity of those who tell us all those venerable tales that we are asked to accept on faith. But there is only one path to true freedom, and so to God. In the end, we must love the Good.

Acknowledgments and Bibliographical Notes

The first three meditations in the second part of this book incorporate lectures that I delivered in the autumn of 2016 at Virginia Theological Seminary, as the inaugural contribution to a newly established series of public addresses endowed by Ms. Margaret H. Costan. I was honored, needless to say, to be the first—though hardly the most distinguished—lecturer in the series, and am still grateful for the hospitality I enjoyed from faculty and students alike during my visit, and for the intelligence and probity with which faculty, students, and visitors responded to my remarks and interrogated my arguments. I am almost afraid to name names, as I am quite likely to be guilty of invidiously forgetting some that I should remember. Still, I have to express my sincerest thanks to the Dean and President of the seminary Ian Markham, Vice-President Melody Knowles, the William Mead Professor in Systematic Theology Katherine Sonderegger, and assistant professor (and Ph.D. candidate) Hannah Mattis for their kindness and unflagging hospitality. Toward the last of these four, I should say, I harbor especially amiable feelings, because she has not only read my fiction, but professes to like it. In my mind, there is no higher virtue than this; her high place among the saints in paradise is already assured. As for all the other delightful persons I met during that visit, I hope it suffices simply to add that I am indebted to them and to everyone else who was involved in the event. I should also note that a somewhat different version of the first of those lectures — or, at least, of its general content — is the one that I delivered in July 2015 at the University of Notre Dame, mentioned in my introduction, under the title "God, Creation, and Evil: The Moral Meaning of *Creatio ex Nihilo*"; the text of that lecture was subsequently published, first in the Fall 2015 issue of *Radical Orthodoxy: Theology, Philosophy, Politics,* and then in my book *The Hidden and the Manifest: Essays in Theology and Metaphysics* (Eerdmans, 2017).

I have dedicated this book to Narcis Tasca, a friend and frequent correspondent, in gratitude for what, to him, was a chance remark, made in passing, but to me was an indispensable reminder not to neglect the issue of orthodox Christology in my Fourth Meditation. He had been annoyed by a Christian philosopher's claim that the real ability freely to reject God absolutely, *in infinitum,* is a necessary dimension of human nature. "Then Christ was not wholly human," was his terse but sufficient answer to the argument. It is obvious, of course, that if there is so much as a single human being who is *personally* incapable of rejecting God, without the fullness of his humanity being thereby impaired, then such a capacity need not logically be a real *personal* possibility for any human being. But the obvious is often so obvious that we fail to remark it, or to mention it if we do.

In this volume, I touch on many of the more conventional discussions of the question of universalism only to the degree that they have some relevance to my project here, and with as little detail as I can get away with. My purpose in these pages, after all, has been to advance my own arguments on the matter, which I regard as sufficiently novel as to make a supporting critical apparatus more or less impossible. So, for anyone interested in the current *status quaestionis* among those Christian philosophers who like to engage in the more traditional lines of debate, I can recommend two books that probably cover the ground about as economically as one could hope. One is Thomas Talbott's *The Inescapable Love of God* (Eugene, OR: Cascade Books, 2014) and the other is John Kronen and Eric Reitan's *God's Final Victory* (New York, London: Bloomsbury Academic, 2013). For those interested in a compendious historical account of ancient and mediaeval Christian universalism, including an all but exhaustive list of the textual sources, two books by the indefatigable patristics scholar Ilaria L. E. Ramelli are worth consulting: *The Christian Doctrine of Apokatastasis* (Leiden, Boston: Brill, 2013) and *A Larger Hope?* (Eugene, OR: Cascade Books, 2018)—though I have to warn readers that the former, having been published by Brill (a press loftily indifferent to the market of general readers), is onerously expensive. Some argue that Ramelli puts too much in when making her case; I disagree, but I can certainly concede that she leaves practically nothing out.

There are only a very few texts quoted in these pages— whether in their original forms or in translation—that require precise citation. In "Doubting the Answers" in Part One, the volume I mention by Brian Davies is *The Reality of God and the Problem of Evil* (London: Continuum, 2006). The epigraph of Part Two of this book is drawn from Isaac of Nineveh (Isaac of Syria), *The Second Part, Chapters IV-XLI*, trans. Sebastian Brock (Leuven: Peeters, 1995), p. 165. The account of Maurice Drury's exchange with Ludwig Wittgenstein recorded at the beginning of my Fourth Meditation can be found in Maurice O'Connor Drury, *Selected Writings of Maurice O'Connor Drury: On Wittgenstein, Philosophy, Religion and Psychiatry* (London, New York: Bloomsbury, 2017), p. 137. The quotation from Eleanore Stump quoted in my Fourth Meditation is from the article "Dante's Hell, Aquinas's Moral Theology, and the Love of God," *Canadian Journal of Philosophy* vol. 16 (1986), pp. 194–195. I confess, however, that I found it in the volume by Kronen and Reitan listed above, and only went looking for the article afterward to make sure I would not misrepresent it. The epigraph to Part Three is drawn from Søren Kierkegaard, *Søren Kierkegaard's Journals and Papers*, vol. 6: *Autobiographical, 1848–1855*, ed. and trans. Howard V. Hong and Edna H. Hong, with Gregor Malantschuk (Bloomington: Indiana University Press, 1978), p. 557.

     All other translations in this text are my own, including (naturally) all quotations from the New Testament.

Index